To John Wels

Wishing you every
possible happiness
and success

Terry Farnsworth
May 1977

On the way up

—the executive's guide to company politics

McGraw-Hill Book Company (UK) Limited

London · New York · St. Louis · San Francisco · Bogotá
Düsseldorf · Johannesburg · Madrid · Mexico · Montreal · New Delhi
Panama · Paris · São Paulo · Singapore · Sydney · Tokyo · Toronto

On the way up

—the executive's guide to company politics
Terry Farnsworth

Drawings by Peter Shepherd

Published by
McGRAW-HILL Book Company (UK) Limited
MAIDENHEAD · BERKSHIRE · ENGLAND

07 084471 2

Library of Congress Cataloging in Publication Data
Farnsworth, Terry.
    On the way up.
    Bibliography: p.
    1. Management. 2. Executives. I. Title.
HD31.F26   658.4   76-2575
ISBN 0-07-084471-2

PRINTED AND BOUND IN GREAT BRITAIN

2 3 4 5 AP 79876

Contents

Preface

Many of the most important things about business are never taught in the business schools. True, you can acquire knowledge and learn techniques but this is barely the tip of the managerial iceberg. Beneath the surface are the things that really count, the skills which will enable you to survive and prosper.

This book is about such skills and how to use them—and how to prevent others from using them on you. It deals with the people you will meet, the situations you will encounter, and shows you how to cope effectively with both. It preaches no sermons and pulls no punches. It deals with reality, not with wishful thinking.

This book cannot guarantee your success in business but it *will* make it harder for you to fail. After reading it you will become more politically sensitive. You will know what goes on behind the scenes. You may not be more able but you will *appear* to be so. In short, it will help you to *make your own luck*.

Acknowledgements

A few of the essays in this book have appeared in modified form in *Management Today*, *The Director*, *Education and Training*, and *600 Magazine* and I am most grateful to the respective Editors for their permission to use them here. I would like to thank Peter Shepherd for so vividly portraying some of the more colourful denizens of the managerial jungle.

Brutus . . . Tis a common proof
That lowliness is young ambition's ladder
Whereto the climber upward turns his face;
But when he once attains the upmost round,
He then unto the ladder turns his back
Looks in the clouds, scorning the base degrees
By which he did ascend.

Shakespeare, *Julius Caesar*, Act II, Scene I

1.

Six steps to executive survival

A living dog is better than a dead lion

Despite the shake-outs of the past few years, many executives continue to believe that they will never be made redundant. And yet time and again it has been proved that neither age nor experience nor seniority nor even competence can provide adequate protection when the axeman cometh. Indeed, during a really ruthless cost cutting drive, the high priced heads are often the first to roll. Make no mistake. Gone are the days when it was sufficient to have been to the right school or to have 'a friend at court'. To stay on the payroll during the turbulent seventies every executive needs a positive strategy for survival. Fortunately, there are a number of well established techniques which, if skilfully used and consistently applied, will virtually guarantee you a place in the team.

K G B (Kill the Good Brains)

Bright, ambitious subordinates must be kept firmly in their place: unchecked, they constitute a potent threat to your survival. To clip the high flyer's wings effectively you need only remember that he thrives upon activity: therefore you must so order things that he is left with practically nothing to do. Avoid delegating anything to him other than the most mundane chores. Feign amnesia when he asks if you have read his latest report. Plead an urgent meeting when he tries to see you. Make sure that no important paperwork ever reaches him until after your decisions have been implemented. And on no account ever ask him for his opinion—this will only encourage him to bore you with his newest inspiration.

After a few months he will be flying lower than a hungry seagull. Indeed, with luck, he may even be transformed into the kind of pliable conformist whose existence you can totally afford to ignore, except perhaps for a gracious word at the office Christmas Party. Even supposing that he still has some initiative left, the chances are that he will apply for a transfer to another department. Needless to say, you will strongly support his application in the interests of his 'career development'. He, in turn, will be piteously grateful, and higher authority will nod approvingly at such evidence of your touching concern for the corporate weal.

Hara-kiri
However benighted he may be, you must not fall into the trap of appearing cleverer than your boss. Acknowledge the reality of his superior fire-power and recognize that his ego is no less sensitive than yours. While you should always avoid a confrontation on any major issue, there is much to be said for stage-managing the occasional 'argument' over a relative triviality, provided that you make certain that you lose. This means taking care beforehand to provide him with all the facts and figures necessary to ensure your downfall, for it is vital that you present him with a sure-fire winner. If, obtusely, he fails to spot the weaknesses in your case, it may even be necessary for you to expose them yourself (with a fine show of momentary confusion or embarrassment).

When finally 'defeated' by your superior, you must, of course, register just the right degree of amazement at his uncanny perceptiveness. Every boss loves a good loser, and sometimes the consolation prizes available to a really good performer—generous salary increases, a larger office, a more impressive job title—can be well worth having. More important still, if you learn your trade well, he will soon regard you as a 'mature' executive with 'positive attitudes' whose presence is an essential prop to his own self-image. To fire you would be unthinkable.

Hunt the minnow
Any executive who wants to stay ahead of the pack must always take

4

care to cultivate his own private intelligence network. To rely upon official company handouts is simply to put oneself at the mercy of the PR department. Many executives go to great lengths to keep on friendly terms with the managing director's secretary in the hope of profiting from the occasional girlish indiscretion. This is a cheap and obvious ploy which is invariably detected—and resented. Nor is it wise to rely wholly upon the grapevine, which all too often consists of a seething mass of fantasies planted by the company's professional wishful thinkers.

The people really worth keeping in with are those who have access to top management but are considered too junior or too disinterested to be capable of appreciating the significance of confidential information, even if it should come into their possession. Such people as tea ladies, filing clerks, office messengers, and company chauffeurs form a kind of privileged elite to whom the normal security precautions do not apply. For example, it would never occur to most executives to keep quiet while the tea is being served at a meeting, even though the subject under discussion may be top secret. Again, it is by no means un-known for a chairman to regale his chauffeur with tit-bits of confidential information to relieve the grinding monotony of a long car journey.

These are the people who are likely to be 'in the know' about the probable location of the company's new factory or to have details of the forthcoming management changes. Nor are they at all unwilling to talk once you have established friendly relations on a day-to-day basis. Accustomed to being patronized or ignored by the majority of execu-tives, they respond quickly to anyone who treats them as normal human beings.

Dynamic inertia
Among the most fashionable precepts of current management theory is the idea that progress means constant, never ending change, both for companies and individuals. At courses and seminars the gospel of 'organizational renewal' is preached with messianic fervour, and whole new departments are created to burrow into existing practices, rethink policies, smooth out anomalies, and generally make life hell for any executive who is not within actual clutching distance of his gold watch. No survival-conscious executive will ever openly resist change since to do so would be to label himself as 'inflexible' or 'uncooperative' and risk being banished to some managerial leper colony north of the Wash. Instead, he follows three simple rules: he is enthusiastic, he takes the initiative, and he lets others do the work.

Any executive who enthusiastically acclaims a new idea put forward by his boss must by definition—his boss's definition—be intelligent. But if he goes further and volunteers his services to see the idea through, then he is unquestionably a man to watch. Volunteering is crucial for a number of reasons. First, it is so rare among executives as to be regarded as an act of almost suicidal bravery; secondly, it relieves the boss himself of the burden of implementation; and finally, most important of all, it enables you to control the rate of progress of the idea and to abort its more unpleasant consequences, especially those which affect you personally.

From then on all will be plain sailing. You will set up 'task forces', convene committees, hold consultations, call for more facts, initiate projects, and occasionally—very occasionally—you will write optimistic memoranda and reports which will convince your boss that yet another major 'breakthrough' has been achieved. Naturally, you will have to allow him to take the credit for all the work which others have done for you, but this is a small price to pay for having reassured him that you still have fire in your belly—and yet pose no threat to his own security.

Uncle Fred

This technique is especially suitable for middle ranking executives who have little prospect of further advancement. While it is essentially a long range strategy, it can be combined very effectively with any of the preceding short range techniques. The object of this approach is to create a company image for yourself which will render you virtually fire-proof. In effect, you aim to be the company's number one do-gooder, a man who is loved by everyone and feared by no one. How can this be done?

Once again, you must stifle your pride and throw yourself enthusiastically into the social life of the organization. There are always plenty of chores around which no one else wants, whether it be acting as MC at the annual company sports, organizing the Christmas Dance, or arranging visits to the theatre for members of the Social Club. Naturally, you will delegate the administrative minutiae to your subordinates while handling all publicity arrangements yourself. However, whenever you are congratulated upon your efforts, especially in public, you will be quick to acknowledge the tremendous help which you have received from every possible quarter, thus eliminating any lurking suspicions that you are just another credit snatcher. Phrases such as 'team effort' and 'combined operation' are particularly potent in producing the desired effect. Within a few years you will find yourself regarded as a

6

kind of corporate Schweitzer. Once beatified in this way, you have a job for life.

Godfather

Many executives think that the best possible insurance against redundancy is to have a highly placed friend or relative in the company. But what if he is fired, or is demoted, or resigns? You will have lost your protector and may even suffer the same fate yourself. It is much better, and safer, to have a few really powerful friends outside the company, the mere mention of whose names is enough to stay the hand of even the most dedicated axeman. But what sort of external contacts should you try to build up? The answer lies in the fact that all companies have a horror of unfavourable publicity: *ergo*, you must cultivate the friendship of those who are in a position to make a fuss. A major shareholder, of course, is always worth having on your side; nor will it hurt if you are known to play golf regularly with several of the firm's most important customers.

However, the really big prizes are those who have the capacity and the means to exert their influence on a national scale—for example, politicians, journalists, and producers of the most astringent type of television documentary. The fact that these gentlemen would, in most cases, be very wary of using their influence directly on your behalf if, say, you were fired, is beside the point: from the company's point of view, there is always a chance that they might, and that is a risk which few companies are willing to take. Organizations, like people, tend to fear the unknown.

One final point. While all of these techniques will help to protect you against redundancy with your present employer, they are not nearly so effective in the event of a takeover or merger. Here there are only two things which you can do: either sit tight and hope for the best, or jump ship. If you do decide to quit, remember that many a displaced executive has found a new lease of life in management consultancy, especially with the type of firm which specializes in 'manpower audits' and 'executive appraisals'. After all, there is always room in business for the man who is motivated to do unto others those things which others have done unto him.

7

2.

Seven deadly sins

No man is demolished but by himself

Thomas Bentley, *A Letter to Mr Pope*, 1735

There are plenty of books on how to get ahead in business but not nearly so many on how easy it is to fail. And yet failure is much more common than success: a few are called to greatness but many are made redundant. Moreover, as every experienced executive knows, success is not simply a matter of competence; one must also know how one is expected to behave.

In every organization there are certain modes of behaviour to which every executive is expected to conform. Failure to comply with these unwritten rules can have a serious effect upon an individual's progress, however able he may otherwise be. Admittedly, just what constitutes unacceptable behaviour can vary considerably from company to company. But there are some types of conduct which are sure to be criticized, even in the most liberal minded concern.

Trespassing

To the outside observer the modern corporation must seem like a Chinese box. For beyond the deceptive simplicities of the company organization chart there lies an apparently endless vista of divisions, groups, departments, and sections, each with its walled-off boundaries and jealously guarded authorities.

At every level in the organization executives fight to defend their boundaries with all the ferocity of jungle predators. Their weapons are job descriptions, organization charts, policy manuals, and procedures which together form a kind of protective minefield against intruders. Let a rival department appear to be trespassing and these mines will be detonated, followed by a withering crossfire of stern memoranda. Life in such companies is like a perpetual civil war in which the battle-field is the company, not the market place.

Often these territorial squabbles penetrate even the humblest levels of the organization. 'It's not my job' becomes as popular a battlecry with typists and tea ladies as among militant machinists and disgruntled electricians. The result is that the company stumbles along like a punch drunk boxer, easy prey for its more disciplined competitors. Especially if they come from Germany or Japan.

Even in the more intimate boss–subordinate relationship, the territorial imperatives are equally strong. There are few surer ways for a man to incur his boss's wrath than to 'go over his head', i.e., communicate directly with higher level management. Such an act immediately sets in motion a whole syndrome of hostility, based largely upon fear and personal insecurity. And yet given a jealous and reactionary boss how else can an enthusiast hope to make his voice heard? It is all very well when the waters flow freely but what happens when the channel is blocked?

Being too independent
If you want to get ahead, don't be too independent: ability without servility is a losing combination. No matter how low your opinion of your boss may be, remember that he is the arbiter of your corporate destiny; without his approval you cannot hope to progress. And if this thought appals you then leave and start your own business. You are unlikely to climb any ladder but your own.

There are a number of ways of checking your Independence Quotient. First, do you tend to go on arguing with your boss after he has made his decision? Afterwards, do you still feel resentful at having been overruled? Do you implement his plan with only lukewarm enthusiasm, while making it clear to others that you expect it to fail? In short, are you totally incapable of losing gracefully? If so, then one thing is certain: the longer you stay the more frustrated you will get.

There is no greater sin in business than to appear too self-sufficient.

It is particularly galling for a boss to feel that you are indifferent to his superior fire-power, that you are more concerned with what rather than with who is right. True, if you are extremely able and would be difficult to replace, you may be left largely to your own devices. But woe betide you when you make mistakes.

Every company tries to generate a kind of corporate patriotism which is intended to foster 'a sense of belonging'. By acting as though you were a member of a one man club you are saying, in effect, that such patriotism is sterile—that you owe no allegiance to anyone but yourself. Naturally, you can hardly expect to be promoted. You will be regarded as a maverick who should stay where he is.

Sexual frolics

One of the quickest ways of descending the executive escalator is to have an affair with your secretary: it is the business equivalent of committing suicide. After all, you are married to the company during office hours and if you are persistently unfaithful she will certainly divorce you. You should also bear in mind that your colleagues will be jealous, especially those who have had their own advances rebuffed.

However discreet you are, the affair is bound to be discovered; after that it will quickly reach the ears of your boss. From then on you will be under close surveillance and even your most trivial errors will be attributed to romantic daydreaming. Your secretary, too, will not escape unscathed. Her colleagues will exchange glances whenever she takes dictation and will greet every interruption with ill concealed delight. It may well be true that 'all the world loves a lover' but *not*, it would seem, during working hours.

By way of contrast, affairs outside the office receive much greater tolerance, especially if the other person involved is not a company employee. 'What a man does in his own time is no concern of ours' is the fashionably liberal viewpoint of most senior executives, anxious to project themselves as men of the world. However, should the affair go sour and begin to affect your work, these permissive attitudes will quickly evaporate. And if you are deluged with emotional phone calls from your former beloved or, worse still, if she should take it into her head to write to your boss, then you will soon be told to 'pull yourself together'. Or else.

Being too creative

There is a great deal of nonsense talked about creativity in business. Indeed, if industry were to accept the views of certain management theorists, every executive would need to be a potential Edison. The truth, of course, is very different. Most organizations find great difficulty in coping with creative people: they have an unfortunate habit of rocking the boat.

To the creative individual nothing is sacred, whether it be existing policies, traditions, methods, or techniques. To strive to change these things not only means that some people will have their routines upset. It also means that they will have to start learning again, with all the effort and potential danger that such a process involves. Remember the more senior or experienced a man is, the greater his commitment to what he already knows. Asking him to acquire new knowledge and skills is like advising a politician to take a course in public speaking. Such advice may be justified but it is unlikely to be welcomed.

Another major problem is that many creative people are abysmal salesmen: they believe that if an idea is good enough it is bound to get through. They have yet to learn a basic precept of infantry warfare, that to attack in mass formation across open country is to invite instant massacre by the enemy's machine guns. More specifically, they need to appreciate that an effective innovator does everything in his power to appear 'one of the boys': he never seeks to make his abilities too obvious. To be so self-effacing may no doubt be a strain but if you want things to change you have little alternative.

Undesirable outside interests
It all depends upon what your interests are. If, for example, you play golf or rugby, then you are merely indulging in the kind of red blooded pursuits which will strengthen your image as a tough minded executive. Conversely, if you are a ballet enthusiast or collect antiques, you may be thought too soft centred to hold high corporate office. This may seem ridiculous and wholly unfair but if you are expecting fairness you ought not to be in business.

Generally speaking, any ball game is acceptable, especially those which involve great physical effort. After all, an ambitious executive needs to keep fit and in preserving your body you are serving the company. Intellectual pursuits are a very different matter. A hobby such as writing, for example, means that you have a proven capacity for independent thought; this, in turn, may lead you to reject those very business values which you are expected to uphold. An interest in politics carries the same potential dangers since you may be seduced by the mismanagement within your own company into believing that the system itself is at fault. Needless to say, if it becomes known that you belong to any left wing organization, then you may as well start clearing your desk immediately. Your days will be as numbered as the leaves in autumn.

Nevertheless, even if you confine your activities to the more robust sports, be sure that you are strong enough to withstand any buffetings. It is no use playing rugby if you are going to be constantly off work with minor injuries; remember, there is no company physiotherapist who is paid to get you fit. Indeed, if it is thought that you are accident prone, you may easily damage your future prospects. It is one thing to have an accident which is an 'act of God' but quite another to suffer injuries which you bring upon yourself.

A misguided sense of humour
Elsewhere in this book it is claimed that a sense of humour will tide you over many of the stresses of executive life. While this is true, you must nevertheless be extremely discriminating in deciding what is funny. For example, if an office junior trips and falls you may roar your head off: if your boss does so then you must act as though it were a personal tragedy.

The art of keeping a straight face even when you are confronted by the most hilarious inanities is—like most worthwhile skills—not easily acquired. It means that you must suspend immediately all your critical faculties and accept even the most ludicrous situation as if it were normal. For example, if one department in a factory is laying off labour which another badly needs, you must see nothing unusual in such a lack of coordination. Similarly, if you are required to fly 500 miles to attend a meeting which begins at noon and finishes after lunch, you must stifle your reservations about its cost effectiveness. Remember, it all happens for the best in the best of all possible worlds. Ask any PRO.

The worst kind of humour to display is the cynical brand because it shows that you have practically no respect for the integrity of management. In other words, your mind is so devious that even if you were given a substantial salary increase you would still suspect that your colleagues were getting more. If this, in fact, is how you would react then there is virtually no hope for you—unless, of course, you are employed to negotiate with trade unions. Every good gamekeeper needs to think like a poacher.

Praising other companies
If you want to make your mark as the company bore, keep talking about the other companies which you have worked for in the past. And if you

aspire to recognition as an executive quisling, make sure that you compare them to your employer's disadvantage. But do not be surprised if it is suggested that you leave. Even the most good natured company has limits to its patience.

It may be, of course, that you are proud of your service with other organizations. Indeed, compared with life in your present company, they may seem like halcyon days when real managers, rather than half-wits, controlled your destiny. Even so, you would be wise not to flaunt your views, particularly if you were recruited from a successful competitor. For while you may have been brought in to inject new ideas, you can hardly expect your colleagues to acknowledge this willingly. After all, if they had been more effective you would not have been needed.

It is best, therefore, to avoid making odious comparisons and to discuss your ideas without ever mentioning that other companies use them. In this way you will not only circumvent any latent company jingoism: you will also be regarded as an original thinker. The time to refer to other companies is when your ideas have been implemented and are working successfully. You can then point out that 'others seem to be following our lead'.

Naturally, if you have previously worked in nationalized industries, you will be considered by everyone to have much to live down. No matter how advanced the technology or humane the personnel policies, you will be unmercifully heckled should you try to sing their praises. Conversely, if you constantly refer to them in disparaging terms, you will be regarded as a man who had the sense to see the light.

Finally, remember that all of these points are merely general guide-lines; there may be other prohibitions which are specific to your company. But make no mistake: the sooner you find out what they are the greater your chances of personal survival. For not everything that matters is to be found in company rule books. The unwritten laws can be just as binding.

3.

Panic stations

But those behind cried 'Forward!'
And those before cried 'Back!'

Macaulay, *Lays of Ancient Rome*
Horatius **XXXI**

Anyone seeking a quiet life should certainly avoid becoming an executive in industry. There are few occupations which subject a man's stamina to more rigorous tests, hence the high rate of failure at the upper echelons. And despite the chidings of management theorists, the executive cannot always be a paragon of rationality. He operates in the real world of human emotions in which logic and reason do not always prevail.

None the less, there are many compensations, not just the material rewards but the satisfactions that come from coping with a multitude of problems, some grand, some trivial, yet all of them requiring a measure of judgement. And if there is one quality above all which a man needs to survive it is a sense of humour; without this almost every problem can seem like a crisis. There are, of course, a number of *bona fide* crises which from time to time afflict even the best run companies. The following are particularly common.

The cost cutting exercise

Sooner or later every company enters a period of recession when sales fall, unit costs rise and those brave-new-world projects are put into cold storage. The more prosperous a company has been, the more traumatic are the effects. Almost overnight ebullient optimists lose their panache and the spectre of redundancy stalks the corridors of power.

It is at times like these that an executive finds out who his friends are and whether his contribution really matters to the company. For make no mistake: every function is on trial for its life and no amount of past success will save those which are judged to be superfluous. It is now that the searchlight is turned upon those non-productive 'service departments'—advertising, public relations, sales promotion, training and, ironically enough, corporate planning. These are the more obvious hostages to fortune who can be cast into the abyss with minimum risk to profits. It is a tempting prospect and one which few companies hesitate to grasp.

Even more solidly based functions soon begin to feel the pinch. Sales forces are decimated, marketing plans are shelved, and vacant offices begin to appear in the personnel department. A wave of puritanical fervour sweeps through the company, engulfing any remaining vestiges of the *dolce vita*. Sales conferences are banned, social functions cancelled, and executives are urged to cut down on client entertainment. Expenses are vetted ruthlessly by power mad accountants and any remaining hedonists are brought quickly into line.

One thing is certain: even if the company survives it will never be the same. Like a city recovering from a devastating earthquake, the remaining corporate citizens emerge warily from their bolt holes, fearful even now that their ordeal may not be over. This is the price which must be paid for a really ferocious cost cutting exercise: the destruction of employee confidence in the company's future. No wonder that so many subsequently vote with their feet and seek a safer refuge from possible future shock.

The flawed image

There are few situations which a company dreads more than a major setback in its public relations, especially if the affair becomes front page news. After all, a company's survival largely depends upon the confidence of others. It must retain not only the support of its customers and shareholders but also the goodwill of its sources of finance.

This is one of the many reasons why the job of top management has become so precarious during the past decade. It needs only one ill starred decision, one lapse of judgement, to erase the achievements of a lifetime of effort—for nothing is more likely to attract the attentions of the media than a seemingly impregnable fortress whose defences have been breached. There is, it would seem, a peculiar satisfaction in seeing the mighty humbled.

All kinds of incidents can trigger off a furore and often it is those which are relatively commonplace that generate the worst publicity. An ill considered sacking which leads to a walkout is generally good for at least a few paragraphs in the popular dailies, especially if the dismissed employee is good 'human interest material', for example has a pregnant wife or is a well known lay preacher or worker for charity. Given such factors as these, the company will receive scant public sympathy, regardless of whether its action was justified. Other sure-fire PR losers include: authorizing layoffs in areas of high unemployment; making unguarded statements about impending redundancies; sleazy divorce cases involving top company executives; and spectacular road accidents caused by hell-driving salesmen. But unquestionably the most damaging publicity of all occurs when a company is publicly accused of cheating its customers by supplying substandard products at premium prices. Let a single hostile question be asked in the House and well groomed heads are virtually certain to roll.

A company which is under attack by the media is like a beleaguered encampment. Staff are forbidden to talk to reporters; meetings are cancelled and conferences postponed; and iron-faced directors hurry to and from the boardroom, trailing PR executives like pilot fish. Eventually comes the news which everyone has been waiting for: X has been fired, Y has resigned, and Z has accepted early retirement. With a sigh of relief the organization goes back to work. The gods have been placated. Life goes on.

The very important visitor

Few things cause greater flutterings in the executive dovecotes than the arrival of a powerful and influential visitor, especially if he turns up at short notice or drops in unannounced. The more dreaded the visitor, the more electric the atmosphere. There is a feeling among executives of being like tethered sheep, awaiting the approach of a marauding tiger.

Nine times out of ten everything goes smoothly and the visitor is steered away from any skeletons in the cupboard. Occasionally, however, things go sadly wrong, particularly if he likes to move around the company and converse democratically with the workers and staff. Sometimes, to the horror of the accompanying senior executives, a well intentioned question to an articulate employee can spark off a tirade which completely 'blows the gaff'. Many a worthwhile improvement has resulted from such encounters and great has been the embarrassment in the executive suite. Thus, it is not those visitors who want to 'see the books' who are most feared. It is those who fancy themselves as 'men of the people'.

There is often a particularly sinister atmosphere in subsidiaries of US multinationals when top corporate executives arrive from the States. Again, it is not so much the set-piece visits, known about for weeks, which cause the biggest panics: it is those which are entirely unexpected. 'Say, I thought I'd just drop in to see you guys as I was passing through London' is a remark which few executives can receive with equanimity. All too often it heralds a spectacular round of cost cutting and 'executive redeployment' which gives a company the appearance of having been sacked by the Goths.

Government visitors and representatives of powerful institutional investors generally receive the most lavish hospitality. In the case of civil servants, no expense is spared since they are thought to spend most of their lives eating in dreary canteens. By way of contrast, visiting American executives are often merely offered sandwiches in the local pub. The reason for this, of course, is not parsimony but politics. Its purpose is to show that management is tightening its belt.

The takeover rumour
Contrary to the beliefs of many boards of directors, not every worker confines his reading to the sports pages of the popular tabloids: some read the city pages too. Indeed the movements of share prices are often watched as avidly by shop floor punters as by the investment managers of unit trusts.

The result is that any city gossip about possible takeovers or mergers is quickly communicated to the toiling masses. In offices and works canteens small but influential groups huddle together to discuss the likely consequences for earnings and jobs. Rumours begin to fly about impending layoffs and the current regulations on redundancy payments receive the same minute scrutiny as the weekly payslip. It is a time of uncertainty when no man feels safe, whether he works on the assembly line or in the front office. And any attempts by management to abort these rumours are doomed to failure. The grapevine is king. Men believe what it says.

Gradually the situation begins to settle down, particularly if the city columns start to make reassuring noises about the prospects for employment. Indeed, it is by no means unknown for opinion within a company to do a complete *volte face* as the potential benefits of the takeover begin

22

to sink in. Naturally, this does not apply when the other company concerned is known to be a 'hire and fire' employer, with an insatiable appetite for 'rationalization'. It is then that there is talk of factory sit-ins and executives begin preparing their *curricula vitae*.

Needless to say, an organization which is in the grip of such rumours cannot hope to function effectively. Productivity plummets, quality suffers, and customer complaints receive scant attention. Nowhere are the effects more marked than at those senior executive echelons where all long term planning grinds to a halt; indeed, even day-to-day decision making may be virtually paralysed. After all, these are men who have no union to protect them and whose re-employment prospects are in many cases bleak. They are, in effect, the last of the feudal retainers, being almost entirely dependent upon their company's patronage. They are like the crew of a ship which has no lifeboats and in which only one man in twenty has ever learned to swim.

The rejected forecast
Every well run company goes through an annual period of gestation which results in its business forecast for the coming year. It is a time of great stress when figures are scrapped, tempers are lost, and late night meetings become the norm. It is ironic that there should be such trauma about a process which amounts to little more than guesswork. But since it has become traditional for companies to peer into the future, most executives regard forecasting as an important task.

The purpose of the forecast is to ensure that the company can make what it can sell and sell what it can make—and that it has the necessary resources to achieve these objectives. It involves the closest cooperation between such ill matched bedfellows as production and marketing, finance and personnel, product PR and corporate research. Eventually, after much toing and froing, and not a little horsetrading, the completed forecast is presented to the board (in US multinationals it is usually vetted by an itinerant circus of high powered hatchet men from the parent company).

But then the blow falls: the forecast is rejected. All concerned must now try again to produce a plan which conforms to their masters' prejudices. Instantly, telephones begin humming between head office and the factories; departmental meetings are convened at short notice; and accountants practise their much needed skills to give the offending figures an acceptable facelift. For those executives in departments at the heart of the maelstrom, the working day becomes intolerably long. Social engagements become out of the question, wives resign themselves to eating alone, and even Saturday morning golf becomes a distant memory. There is only one thing that matters in life: getting that—forecast through, whatever the cost.

Sometimes this whole cycle is repeated two or three times until at last the board gives way through sheer fatigue. At once a kind of carnival atmosphere grips the organization and lifelong enemies nod affably in the lifts. Within a few days, many executives have gone on holiday, leaving their deputies behind to tidy up the details. For another year at least life resumes its normal tempo. Soon, those lifelong enemies cease to nod affably in the lifts.

The wildcat strike

In any situation where there is a conflict of interest, be it a trial of strength or a test of skill, it is inevitable that some contestants will try to bend the rules—or to ignore them completely if the stakes are high enough. This is a fact of life which is often overlooked by moralizing politicians. It is all very well to declaim your faith in the 'working man' but what do you do when some of them try to cheat?

Many wildcat strikes are essentially attempts to cheat, to take by force that which reasoned argument might deny. They are invariably carefully timed to cause maximum inconvenience, to the company, its customers, and the general public. The effect upon the firm is, of course, direct and brutal. If nothing is being produced, nothing can be sold and in competitive markets the opposition has a field day. The spectacle of a once proud lioness being savaged by hyenas is not the most endearing of nature's spectacles, especially when the attackers are being assisted by her cubs. Yet such is the reality in business terms.

The usual response of management is to keep plugging away despairingly like a tired bowler who is being hit to the boundary with monotonous frequency. Meetings are held, proposals are made, and tight lipped 'no comments' snapped at lurking reporters. In the case of a prolonged stoppage, harassed executives appear on TV to be interrogated at length by 'impartial' interviewers—often men who know nothing about business and care even less. Meanwhile, back at the stricken factory, efforts are concentrated upon retaining the firm's customers and miracles of improvization are performed every day. The Dunkirk spirit flares once again but this time the enemy is within the gates.

Suddenly, like a fever, the crisis is past. Assembly lines hum, lorries come and go, and life resumes its unglamorous routine. But the cost has been heavy and the casualties high. Wages have suffered, customers have defected, and already there is talk of jobs being lost. It has been a suicidal contest which no one has won. And yet everyone knows that it will happen again.

There is, of course, a whole pantheon of minor crises with which every executive learns to cope: the missing file which the boss needs in five minutes flat; the projector which fails during a crucial presentation; the visiting speaker who misses his train; the puncture on the way to an important customer. These things can sometimes evoke yearnings for a more peaceful life. But this is what business is all about. Only he that endureth shall collect his pension.

4.

Management's secret techniques

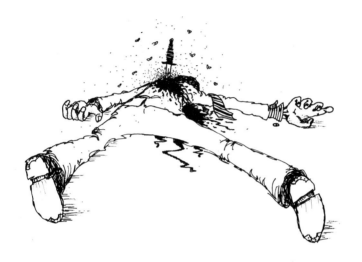

O put not your trust in princes

Psalms cxlvi. 2

Of all the techniques which have rained down upon managers during the past decade none has had more impact than Management by Objectives. Indeed, so great has been the success of MBO that other proven strategies are being gravely underutilized. The problem is especially acute in the case of young business graduates who are still in the throes of their managerial apprenticeship. Frequently, such men have a surfeit of knowledge, but only a modicum of ringcraft, and need greater exposure to the realities of management. Here then are seven alternatives to MBO which no man of ambition can afford to ignore. Judiciously selected and discreetly applied, they will add breadth and perspective to existing skills.

Management by coercion
According to this, mankind can be divided into two basic categories: all powerful leaders who must be unquestioningly obeyed and cloth headed subordinates, idle to the core, who can only be motivated by fear of the sack. Since most modern managers see themselves as liberal and enlightened, this somewhat primitive approach is now distinctly unfashionable; indeed, only a few dinosaurs still espouse it openly.

Still, in management, the fact that a philosophy is out of favour does not mean that it is dead: it simply means that its disciples must use more subtlety. For example, while it is rare for a boss to fire a man just because he dislikes him, there is nothing to prevent him from withholding a salary increase, or from deleting the man's name from a promotion shortlist. Again, should he wish to get rid of a really troublesome individual, he need only restructure the man's job so that his weaknesses are exposed. The subsequent dismissal then becomes a mere formality, and invariably the boss will be commended for his vigilance.

Management by conversion

By all means hitch your wagon to a rising executive: but be ready to jump off if he begins to falter. The signs of a downward trend in your patron's fortunes are usually unmistakable—frequent absences on training courses; his sudden reassignment to a 'consultancy' role; and, most sinister of all, the dismemberment of his empire into smaller units (the old Roman technique of 'divide and conquer'). As soon as the vultures start to gather, it is time to nail your colours to some other mast. Discreetly, you will begin to air your 'reservations' about your patron's policies. You will stay silent at meetings when he is expecting your support. And during casual conversation with his most bitter opponents, you will confess to a growing disenchantment.

By the time the blow falls on the unfortunate, conversion to the other camp should be virtually complete. And far from being spurned as a renegade or turncoat, you will be welcomed to the fold like the Prodigal Son. But beware; the price of survival is eternal vigilance. Always keep your ear pressed firmly to the ground. Only those who are poised on the brink of retirement can afford to be insensitive to political currents.

Management by desertion

This technique will bring peace to any executive who may be worrying about the possibility of a breakdown caused by overwork. If practised consistently, it will virtually guarantee your pension. If you are becoming overwhelmed by your problems, the answer, of course, is to delegate. Stop toting that barge, cease lifting that bale, and recognize that, if you were to expire tomorrow, you could be replaced without causing anything more serious than a few minor ripples on the corporate duckpond.

Every manager needs time to recharge his batteries, so have no qualms about delegating your more mundane chores. After all, one of your key responsibilities is to develop your subordinates, and there is no substitute for experience which is gained on the job. Moreover, you can use the time saved to engage in more important activities, like planning the recruitment of additional staff. Many executives have soared to great heights through their prowess as delegators; indeed, some are always in demand as chairmen at management conferences. Only a few have been careless enough to get fired or made redundant.

Naturally, like any good thing, delegation can be overdone, and you must keep up the appearance of being fully committed. However, this particular problem is easily overcome: simply insist upon regular written reports on practically everything which you delegate. The resulting pile of paperwork upon your desk will create the impression that you are a veritable human dynamo. Needless to say, only a small proportion of this material need actually be read.

Management by diversion
In the days of ancient Rome, the uncouth masses were diverted from their miseries by the skilful use of popular entertainments such as gladiatorial contests. In modern companies such needs are catered for by generous fringe benefits and recreational facilities. There is something here for everyone. The dissatisfied executive may not have much of a job, but at least he has a pension. The worker on the assembly line, however bored, can look forward to the Thursday evening darts match at the company club. Secretaries can make new friends at the lunch-time disco or over a game of ping-pong. Long serving stalwarts, close to retirement, can browse among the newspapers in the office library.

Never underestimate the power of such diversionary strategies: they have taken the steam out of many a tense situation. After all, it is difficult to go on hating that young idiot in Accounts if you partner him at golf in the Chairman's Cup. Likewise, the occasional lunch with a hard pressed secretary will convince her that her labours have not been in vain. American owned companies are particularly keen on 'diversion' since it offers many opportunities to promote 'employee togetherness'. Indeed, in some organizations there is a never ending spate of dances and outings which (it is hoped) encourage staff to 'identify' with the corporate juggernaut.

Management by perversion
Simply the art of tailoring any communication to meet your own personal needs. It is not what you say, but what you leave unsaid that is important; not what you put in, but what you leave out. This technique is frequently employed by company chairman at annual general

31

meetings; there are plenty of other less exalted applications. For example, many 'performance appraisal interviews' are not nearly as objective as their supporters claim; indeed, some are mere exercises in manipulation. The strategy used by 'appraisers' at these discussions is invariably the same: keep the man interested and highly motivated, but never commit yourself to anything specific. Thus, many an employee is assured that his 'long term prospects' are excellent, simply because he would be difficult to replace.

A similar approach is practised by some graduate recruiters to entice promising young fledglings into the company's net. Amazing fantasies are sometimes woven about the glittering opportunities awaiting management trainees. The fact that these tactics result in disillusionment and turnover is conveniently overlooked. After all, such losses can always be blamed upon the training department. But do not feel too badly about using this technique: most men would hate to see themselves as others see them. Always remember that truth is a mistress who can be loved too well.

Management by submersion
As every wise manager knows, the road to redundancy is paved with good ideas. Despite all the conference cant about initiative and creativity, it is safer to have no ideas at all if you wish to survive. By doing as you are told and plodding on regardless you pose no threat to anyone and can merge into the background. Soon you will be regarded as a harmless decoration who is no more dangerous than a potted plant in the open plan office.

Unfortunately, as a manager, you will be expected to change things occasionally and to change without changing requires no little skill. Sometimes you can take the lead yourself: for example, a few trivial adjustments to your departmental records system can be sold to your boss as a major innovation. More often, however, you will find yourself embroiled in changes sparked by others, and it is frequently unwise to be openly critical. Far better to pledge your support, do the minimum that is necessary, and emerge virtually unscathed when the storm has passed. Make no mistake: enthusiastic words and apathetic deeds can undermine even the most radical changes. But be sure that it is safe before you revert to 'business as usual'. To revert prematurely could leave you dangerously exposed.

Management by subversion
This is particularly favoured by frustrated executives who seek to

punish their companies for their lack of advancement. Such men are especially active in large organizations where there are strong traditions of corporate paternalism. The attitudes of these internal 'freedom fighters' are easily defined. First, a total disbelief of all company publicity; secondly, a profound suspicion of higher management; and finally an unshakable conviction that 'pull', not performance, is the key to success. For them the corporation is a malignant force which can only be defeated by guerilla tactics: hence most of their battles are fought in corridors and washrooms.

Many of these men are disappointed promotion seekers; others are former 'high flyers' imprisoned by jealous bosses in meaningless jobs. As a result, they regard it as their duty to 'straighten out' anyone who shows respect for company policies, especially those relating to promotion and career development. Cynical as they are, such men are easy to work for. Being anarchists at heart, they tend to regard almost any mistake with a kind of tolerant amusement which often merges into sheer indifference. Essentially, they are rebels who have found their cause: the progressive undermining of the firm's corporate image.

One final point. Remember, you can adapt any of these strategies to MBO: the principles involved are exactly the same. For example, you can devise objectives for coercing your opponents just as easily as for any other part of your job. You can set 'diversionary' objectives for improving the morale of your staff (departmental luncheons are a useful ploy). You can even create more time for 'desertion' by delegating more conventional targets to ambitious young thrusters. After all, they need the experience more than you do. Curiously enough, however, few of these techniques are ever mentioned in the management textbooks; nor are they taught at the business schools; but, make no mistake, managers are adept at learning these techniques where all the most effective management training takes place—on the job.

5.

Take me to your leader

They say best men are moulded out of faults,
And, for the most, become much more the better
For being a little bad.

Shakespeare, *Measure for Measure*, Act IV, Scene V

The chief executive is popularly viewed as a kind of managerial Superman, the incarnation of every business virtue. In books and articles and at seminars and conferences he is portrayed as a blend of decision maker and visionary, a mini-Napoleon with overtones of Moses. The truth is, of course, that he is no less fallible than any other executive; he is simply the victim of a business myth. And far from being a rather bloodless stereotype, he is endearingly human in his strengths and weaknesses.

The Ditherer

Not every chief executive is a dynamic decision maker—there are some who dread having to make up their minds. Such men are found mainly in large organizations which are strongly entrenched in their specialized markets and have little to fear from their much weaker competitors. They are virtually unknown in small and medium sized firms where their talents would result in speedy bankruptcy.

The Ditherer is a man who has had greatness thrust upon him, a reluctant bridegroom in a shotgun marriage. He is nearly always the outcome of a boardroom power struggle, a compromise candidate between two warring factions. Having been too indecisive to support either group, he found to his amazement that he was acceptable to both. Naturally, each side hoped that he could be easily manipulated, like some medieval monarch at the mercy of his barons.

Unfortunately, what neither group reckoned with was his infinite capacity to procrastinate. Being temperamentally averse to committing himself, the Ditherer is a master of delaying tactics with a well stocked armoury of bureaucratic weapons which he uses to defend himself against the need to choose. For him there is no problem which cannot benefit from further 'research' or from an 'in depth study' by a working party. By the time that these bodies have presented their reports, the moment for action has usually passed.

No matter how successful an organization may have been, the Ditherer can be relied upon to bring it to its knees. Fuming with frustration, the best men leave and only sycophants and mediocrities stay behind. Gradually a kind of paralysis grips the company as the rudderless vessel heads straight for the rocks. But even now the Ditherer runs true to form—instead of manning the lifeboats he goes down with the ship.

The Front Man

Like the Ditherer, the Front Man is boss in name only; he is invariably the pawn of his more powerful colleagues. Often an impressive figure with a senatorial air, his value lies not in his managerial talents but in his ability to create confidence in the company's future. Frequently a peer or a retired general, he is prized for his contacts in the City and in government and brings 'a touch of class' to the corporate image.

Nevertheless, a pawn he is and a pawn he remains; he is rarely privy to the Board's real intentions. Having neither the taste nor the ability for day-to-day decision making, he relies heavily upon his more numerate colleagues and is easily manoeuvred into taking their advice. The real power rests with the financial men whom the Front Man holds in considerable awe. He is only too willing to delegate the 'nitti-gritti' since he believes that his job is to concentrate upon 'strategy'. Being basically a simpleton in business matters, the Front Man is no match for the more ruthless power players. Should the company's fortunes suffer a serious setback, he makes the perfect scapegoat for angry shareholders and is usually much too gentlemanly to put up a fight. A sadder and somewhat wiser man, he may reflect with some bitterness upon a great business truth: it is often easier to handle one's external competitors than to deal with enemies who are within the gates.

The Inheritor

Here is a man who owes everything to his father who built up the firm and handed him the crown. Found almost exclusively in small family businesses, the Inheritor is usually either an utter wastrel or an extremely competent, hard working executive. If he is the former then the firm will quickly go broke; if the latter it will often show amazing growth.

However, regardless of his abilities, the Inheritor is a man with a distinctive philosophy which is perhaps best described as benevolently autocratic. He is convinced that workers are merely overgrown children who need guidance in recognizing where their interests lie. Profoundly anti-union and 'agin big government', he rules the firm as though he were a feudal landlord and his employees a band of subservient tenants. He will have no truck whatever with 'worker participation' which he simply equates with communist subversion. His ideas on leadership are equally clear: it is for him to give orders and others to obey.

Yet despite his authoritarian tendencies, the Inheritor's bark is much worse than his bite. He prides himself upon knowing his employees individually and is always ready to help with any personal problems. Again, he is the least machiavellian of men and will rarely engage in any subterfuge. This largely explains his popularity with his workers who regard him basically as a harmless eccentric.

The Bon Viveur

This man believes in enjoying himself: he is all booze and birds and executive lunches. Having worked extremely hard to reach the top, he feels fully entitled to the spoils of office and is a lavish spender of the company's money. Yet for all his extravagance he has impeccable taste; his luxurious office with its original paintings makes a perfect setting for receiving merchant bankers.

His most important task, he feels, is to keep up appearances—to project the image of a successful company. Accordingly, he takes pride in his membership of exclusive clubs and in addressing the head waiters by their Christian names. He loves to be photographed in chic Mayfair restaurants, preferably in the company of a well known peer. He is also to be seen in fashionable nightclubs, often with a lady who is not his wife.

Nevertheless, his life is not all champagne and caviar; he still retains his shrewd business brain. He is an excellent judge of executive talent and promotes ambitious young thrusters into key positions. He has no time whatever for yes-men and theorists and can sometimes be ruthless in axing them. And as many an accountant has found to his cost, he can read a balance sheet just as well as a wine list.

The Hit Man

One of the most unpleasant types of chief executive, the Hit Man is riddled with psychotic tendencies. Having achieved his position through a talent for treachery, he lives in a world of fear and suspicion, trusting no one and doubting all. He insists on taking every major decision and regards delegation as a sign of weakness. Far from developing a competent successor, he makes it his business to drive good men out.

The result is that the company is gradually denuded of talent and this eventually begins to affect its results. For the Hit Man, however, there is a simple explanation: he is surrounded by fools who are not pulling their weight. He therefore initiates yet another purge and desperately tries to recruit new men. Needless to say, they do not stay long once they discover that their authority is nil. The cycle begins all over again and the firm slides nearer and nearer the abyss.

A creature of rapidly shifting moods, the Hit Man's behaviour is totally unpredictable. One moment he is bubbling with bonhomie, the next he can be as vicious as a rattlesnake. The only permanent factor in his mental makeup is his suspicion that people are plotting against him and that he is about to be toppled by a boardroom coup. Ironically, it is this kind of self-induced stress which often results in his ultimate downfall. He often succumbs to a coronary or a breakdown while attempting to fight off a takeover bid.

The Aristocrat

Found mainly at the helm of blue chip British companies, the Aristocrat is the doyen of chief executives. With his Oxbridge background and cultured accent, his faultless tailoring and surface charm, he is more like a successful diplomat than a hard headed practising businessman. But make no mistake: he is the complete professional. There is fire in his belly, not merely gin and tonic.

Not surprisingly, given the size of the company he leads, he often becomes an important public figure and frequently takes part in television discussions. With his urbane manner and polished delivery, he is the perfect representative of enlightened capitalism and can always be relied upon to remain cool and constructive even when faced by the most hostile interviewer. Having spent most of his life manipulating people, he relishes the challenge of the situation which he sees as an opportunity to demonstrate his skills. He answers every question with statesmanlike dignity and takes a moderate position on every issue.

But back at the office he can be anything but a moderate, particularly in times of economic stress. When profits are falling he becomes a ruthless executioner for whom loyalty and long service have little significance. Naturally, he never talks about 'sacking' an executive but merely of having to 'let him go'. Similarly, he never speaks of 'worker redundancies' since 'releasing resources' sounds more public spirited.

The Iceberg

The Iceberg is a kind of human computer, a highly numerate 'figure man' for whom everything can be valued in pounds and pence. Often the product of a business school, he runs his company with clinical efficiency and is excellent at spotting outstanding young talent. Being totally committed to expanding the business, he regularly puts in a sixteen hour day and expects those who work for him to be equally dedicated.

A shy, retiring figure, he has an intense dislike of personal publicity and will rarely consent to be interviewed by the press. At such company functions as he is forced to attend, he will often make only the briefest of appearances, reading his speech as though it were a funeral oration before scuttling back to the safety of his office. And yet for all his asceticism, he commands respect and sometimes even a kind of pity. He obviously gets so little fun out of life that even his subordinates begin to feel sorry for him.

Such feelings are generally short lived for the Iceberg is the most demanding of business taskmasters. He is totally indifferent to domestic considerations and drives his executives like a chain gang overseer. Meetings are called late in the afternoon which frequently go on far into the night and woe betide any man who asks to be excused. Working for him is not just a full time vocation; it is a perfect recipe for a broken marriage.

The Optimist

Uninhibited and extrovert, the Optimist is the 'follow me' type of leader who loves to be in the thick of every business battle. He regards it as his job to inspire his troops and is usually very popular with all levels of employees. He is most commonly found in sales oriented companies which operate in highly competitive markets. Such firms are frequently American owned, though the Optimist himself is normally British.

The Optimist makes an ideal leader in an economic boom since his natural instinct is to keep going forward. Unfortunately, when a recession sets in, his strongest virtues tend to work against him and he is often slow to react to a deteriorating situation. Since cost cutting and retrenchment are anathema to him, he gamely tries to continue advancing, only to find that he is running short of cash. In many ways he is a stubborn, Canute-like figure who has yet to learn that willpower is not always enough.

Soon, of course, cries of alarm and displeasure begin to be heard in the States and grim faced accountants are sent to investigate. Within hours of their arrival all recruitment is stopped and advertising budgets are mercilessly slashed. The whole company undergoes a prolonged inquisition and those found wanting are removed from their jobs. The Optimist is naturally among the first to go, a general who never knew when to retreat.

However, there is one type of chief executive who seems to thrive upon disaster—the resilient, ever-fortunate Rolling Stone. This is the kind of man who, despite having failed in company after company, moves smoothly and effortlessly into yet another top job. It is as though he were being guarded by some beneficent deity so great is his ability to turn defeat into victory. But let us not begrudge him his capacity for survival. If such men can prosper there is hope for us all.

6.

The company courtiers

We are the hollow men
We are the stuffed men
Leaning together

T. S. Eliot, *The Hollow Men*

There has never been a shortage of fantasies about what goes on inside the boardroom of a large corporation. Many people who have never worked in industry imagine it to be a kind of secular Vatican where grim faced executives spend their time deliberating the great eternal issues of profit and loss. For others, less kindly disposed to business, it is simply a battleground for rival conspiracies, a place where plot meets counter-plot and where men's careers are broken in the merciless struggle for money and power. Still other critics, noting the ripe ages of many directors, conclude that it is merely a more opulent version of an old people's home in which geriatric executives, long past their prime, grapple vainly with problems which are beyond their reach.

There are, of course, elements of truth in all of these fantasies. There *are* plots, there *are* conspiracies, there *is* power play—what else would you expect from men who have climbed so high? Nevertheless, with few exceptions, the average boardroom is neither a cosy club nor a ruthless charnel house: it is an updated version of a medieval court. Here, monarch of all he surveys, sits the chairman; at his right hand, his chancellor and confidant, the managing director. Grouped around them are the principal courtiers, some brash and extrovert, some cautious and withdrawn, all of them dedicated to the corporate weal. While the temperaments of such men are as varied as their backgrounds, every board contains at least one of the following types.

The Court Jester

Industry is full of comedians, ranging from the unconscious humour of the PR man, who understandably believes his own press releases, to the professional cynic for whom all such material reads like a Marx Brothers script. Every board has a Jester and the type of humour which he displays is directly related to the company's environment. For example, the Jester on the board of a 'blue chip' merchant bank will invariably be given to dry, waspish innuendoes, often laced with classical allusions; his counterpart in a tough minded marketing company is more likely to favour the kind of humour found in working men's clubs.

Devoid though he may be of the traditional pigskin bladder and cap and bells, the modern Court Jester performs essentially the same function as his medieval ancestor. He pricks pomposities, punctures egos, debunks the charlatan, and comforts the depressed. With one well timed quip he can quell a digression, deflate a bore, or infuse warmth and common sense into the sourest atmosphere.

So long as he retains the affection of his chairman, he enjoys an almost unlimited freedom to practise his skills. But woe betide him if one of his enemies should succeed to the throne. His head is usually among the first to roll.

The Young Pretender

As a result of the admittedly fading vogue for thrustful young whizzkids, many companies find themselves with such men on their boards. Despite their youth and relative inexperience, some organizations regard them as powerful aphrodisiacs, capable of instantly restoring a company's potency. The typical 'Young Turk' is, of course, brimming with self-confidence and is no respecter of corporate tradition. Armed to the teeth with the latest management jargon, he rampages through the firm like a berserk witch doctor, sniffing out problems (even where none exist), terrifying the natives with his razor sharp questions, and summarily executing various sacred cows.

Naturally, he is disliked by his less dynamic associates since such boundless energy is always hard to forgive. But he is invariably treated with discretion and respect, since he is seen to be in the running for the MD's chair. The real test of his strength comes when he makes his first big mistake. It is then that he finds himself in the middle of a howling wolf pack, eager to tear him limb from limb.

This is the kind of battle which he cannot win, for even if he survives his escutcheon will have been tarnished and he will have lost the aura of infallibility which is his greatest asset. And so, after pouring out his troubles to various sympathetic headhunters, he eventually sets sail for friendlier shores, where history repeats itself all over again.

The Eminence Grise

The most natural contender for the role of kingmaker is the personnel director, because of his unlimited access to employee records. Moreover, he is generally at the centre of a complex intelligence network which provides him with a regular flow of information on managers' peccadilloes. Unfortunately, since he regards it as his duty to keep the MD well briefed, he is sometimes regarded by his colleagues with considerable suspicion.

Nevertheless, given his day-to-day contacts with the highest echelons, only the most foolhardy executive will choose to make an enemy of him. Indeed, the majority take great pains to keep on good terms. Paradoxically, despite his influence, it is rare for a personnel director to become the top man: he seems forever doomed to be a spectator at the wedding.

This is because he is often regarded by his masters as 'too clever by half' and unlikely to be acceptable to his more forthright colleagues. There is, of course, an element of truth in this charge since subtlety is part of his stock in trade.

Be that as it may, the best type of personnel director, being a skilled manipulator, exerts a civilizing influence upon his more autocratic associates and can usually deal competently with even the tensest situation.

The War-Lord

Nearly every board has its War-Lord: the kind of tough, cynical pragmatist who believes (not without reason) that he who shouts loudest gets the most notice. Possessed as he is by an almost Hitlerian urge to dominate and subdue, he operates at board meetings like a one man Vesuvius, now apparently dormant, now erupting furiously against any fancied encroachments upon his territorial boundaries.

Here is a man who makes a virtue of ignorance and who regards any idea not generated by himself as a direct challenge to his managerial virility. His particular *bêtes noires* are those so-called 'staff departments' whose denizens he regards as profit eating locusts with an insatiable appetite for bureaucratic interference. However successful he may be at 'getting the production out' or in achieving his sales forecasts, he is a major long term threat to the prosperity of his company since, being opposed to delegation and any form of training, he surrounds himself exclusively with sycophants and yes-men.

The result is that when he resigns, retires, or finally succumbs to paranoia, he leaves behind, not a rich variety of executive saplings, lovingly nurtured for just such a day, but a vast managerial wilderness, devoid of talent, which becomes a permanent drain on the company's profitability.

The Gentleman-in-Waiting

There is no mystery about what this executive is waiting for: he longs only for the lush pastures of retirement when at last he can begin to make amends for all those wasted years in the service of Mammon. Often a gentle, cultured figure who prefers to stand aloof from the frenetic power play of his more ambitious colleagues, he radiates the calm, senatorial dignity of the 'born' elder statesman.

Since he appears to pose no threat to anyone, he is universally liked and his advice is often sought when coronaries and incompetence create the occasional vacancy at the boardroom table. In fact, he is no less fallible in his judgements than any other executive and will invariably recommend a civilized mountebank who has been to the right school in preference to an earthy vulgarian with a talent for making money. In this way, given enough time and sufficient influence, he can totally undermine that diversity of human types which is the inner strength of any effective board.

However, since it frequently takes several years before the corporate engine finally breaks down, he usually manages to escape the worst consequences of his own advice by retiring conveniently to some idyllic retreat, blissfully unaware of the havoc which he has wreaked.

The Keeper of the Purse

There is no more misunderstood figure in the boardroom than the financial director: he is the one member who is constantly criticized for doing his job. As the company's number one 'no-man', he is inevitably cast in the role of either cheese-parer-extraordinary, or brutal executioner of new ideas.

Not surprisingly, his never ending skirmishes with the company's financial libertines tend to leave their mark and he is rarely noted for his bubbling sense of humour. Nevertheless, being one of the few members of the board who is comfortable with figures, he can sometimes run rings around his less numerate colleagues and it is exceptional for him to suffer a major defeat.

His most serious drawback as an executive is his insensitivity to human problems and his tendency to see such issues in black and white terms. There is no doubt, however, that he is worth his weight in gold, so long as he is kept at a respectful distance from the driver's seat. Possessing little taste or capacity for inspirational leadership, he is often more renowned for his attacks upon costs than for his creative contributions to corporate strategy.

The Steward

You can always recognize the Steward on the board: he is the professional flatterer who tries unavailingly to be everyone's friend. It is a miracle that he has risen so high since he is clearly ill at ease in practically any situation except the Christmas Dance. Here at last he can shine as a dispenser of *risqué* jokes and his own characteristic brand of back-slapping bonhomie.

He has long since steeled himself to accept the slings and arrows of his fellow directors and seems to take an almost masochistic pleasure in being the boardroom punchbag. His craving for popularity is not so much a personality trait as a reflection of his fear of being 'found out' since he is nearly always the product of overpromotion. Lacking any real ability, he relies for his protection upon winning the friendship of his more powerful associates whom he mistakenly feels would never countenance his removal. Many men of his type were, of course, axed during the executive purges of the early seventies and some are still haunting the employment agencies, bitterly regretting their misplaced trust.

The real villain of the piece is not the Steward himself but the man who promoted him and so thrust a degree of greatness upon him that he was unable to bear. A man more to be pitied than despised, the Steward is a member of a dying breed, ground between the millstones of technological change and the exacting demands of professional management.

The Monarch

Finally, what kind of Monarch is best suited to reign over such men: what are the qualities of the ideal chairman? Certainly it will help if he is reasonably bright—but not so bright that his colleagues are inhibited from speaking their minds. And even if this is not a problem, and for some chairmen it is not, he will still have to master the art of appearing alert and interested when he is paralytically tired and thoroughly bored. But above all he needs the hunter's instinct for approaching danger and the kind of personal radar which can penetrate verbiage and detect the self-interest that lies beneath.

And all the time he must keep a weather eye upon his fellow Monarchs in other kingdoms who, armed with takeover bids or merger proposals, will be only too ready to invade should he begin to falter. But as it has always been, so shall it always be. Uneasy rove the eyes that scan the balance sheet.

7.

On the way up

There is always room at the top

Daniel Webster

Despite the indifferent performance of British industry during the past two decades, it would be nonsense to suggest that there is any shortage of executive talent. On the contrary, there are hundreds of dynamic, thrustful, creative executives in almost every sector of our business life. The curious thing is that relatively few of them reach the top. Indeed, for every high flyer who reaps his just reward there are whole platoons of mediocrities who are equally successful.

How have they done it? Certainly not by exploiting their natural gifts or most of them would, in racing terms, still be under starter's orders. The truth is that they have learned to play the game according to the rules, rules which do not appear in any textbook, nor in the syllabus of any management course. Yet they are far more effective than any MBA in ensuring a trouble free ride to the top.

Keep a low profile
Every institution creates its own myths and management is no exception. For example, judging by the euphoric tone of the executive appointment columns, one might imagine that there is an insatiable demand for 'men of vision and initiative', capable of revitalizing even the most deadbeat organization.

Not so. To survive and prosper, particularly in large corporations, it is necessary that you acquire the art of keeping your head down and your shoulder to the wheel—an uncomfortable posture but one which will pay off in the end. In other words, you must cultivate a kind of professional anonymity, while at the same time taking care to conform to all the various tribal rituals and unwritten laws, which are designed to mould you into the corporate image. Indeed, keep your ego firmly in check and you will go further than all those rumbustious whizzkids who arrive with a bang and resign with a whimper.

There is, however, one area in which you can scarcely have too much visibility: in-company sporting activities. For example, if there is a company golf club, join it at once: many a man's career has been made at the 19th hole. Similarly, if you are good at cricket or rugger, then exploit your talents to the full, while remaining suitably modest about any successes which you achieve. Of course, not all games are of equal value; indeed a talent for one of the more cerebral pastimes such as chess may simply mark you out as a dangerous intellectual. You should also avoid games like darts and ping-pong which are regarded as far too 'down-market' for an aspiring executive.

Don't be a maverick

Having joined a company, many executives feel that they have to prove themselves and begin generating paperwork like berserk computers. So long as such material is clearly marked 'for information only' no great harm is done. But if you persist in upsetting your colleagues by expecting them actually to welcome and even to implement your ideas, then you are in for a frustrating time. The sooner you learn that new ideas, by definition, threaten the *status quo*—and therefore the security of your boss and colleagues—the more quickly you will ascend the executive escalator. Recognize from the start that the only ideas worth supporting are those which come *down* to you. Those which come *up* to you are merely the fantasies of fools.

When you can steel yourself to congratulating your boss upon his latest inspiration (albeit an idea which you mentioned to him six months ago) then you will have achieved that degree of self-discipline which is a prerequisite of success. But if you experience feelings of resentment and would like to grasp him by the throat, then make no mistake: you are still serving your executive apprenticeship.

Remember too, that an ambitious executive can never afford to be off his guard, even in the relaxed setting of a pub or the company restaurant. Exercise the greatest care when expressing your views on any issue which is likely to be controversial. It is, of course, perfectly in order for you to make patronizing comments about the Government and there is never a close season so far as Mrs Whitehouse is concerned. Apart from such obvious targets, however, tread warily or you may begin to be thought of as being too dogmatic and inflexible to hold high office in the company. After all, if you were to become chairman or managing director, you would not always be able to pick and choose your outside contacts. On the contrary, you would have to be prepared to cultivate any which might benefit the company's interests, even though some of them might conflict with your own personal beliefs. Thus, many an MD who is a pillar of his local Conservative Association takes pride in his friendships with prominent trade unionists. To be too rigidly partisan would simply be bad for business.

Project the right image
Unless you work in advertising or PR, in which case your bow ties and coloured shirts will be accepted as natural occupational flamboyance, you would be well advised to dress conservatively. A charcoal grey suit, white shirt, and an innocuous tie will not only proclaim your sartorial fitness for the executive club: they will also hint at underlying qualities of reliability and discretion. By all means wear the company tie, if one exists, but—unless you are employed in the City—resist the temptation to wear those of your old school or regiment. In industry, such insignia are regarded as evidence of social elitism and may arouse feelings of resentment and jealousy among your less privileged associates. It is also a mistake to copy your boss's turnout since he will almost certainly regard this as impudence, not flattery, and as a clear indication that you do not know your place.

But wearing the right clothes is only part of the problem: you must also learn to communicate in an acceptable fashion. Use the word 'I' as infrequently as possible and avoid making blunt statements of opinion which could leave you with little room to manoeuvre. Instead of saying 'I strongly recommend', try something more restrained and diplomatic like 'ought we not perhaps to consider?' By communicating in such an acceptably low key, you will quickly acquire a reputation for far sighted statemanship which will be worth its weight in gold in the promotion stakes.

Similarly, in your choice of personal possessions, you should aim at projecting an image of solid, bourgeois respectability, not one of provocative affluence. Even if your wife has a private income, you should never permit her to drive a Rover when it is common knowledge that the chairman's wife has only a Mini. Another stern test comes when you invite your boss to dinner for rest assured that his wife will be making a mental inventory of everything that she sees. And woe betide you if your dinner service is more expensive than hers, your furniture more comfortable, and your pictures more tasteful. The subsequent financial Dunkirk which your boss will have to face will certainly not make you one of his favourite sons.

Be a good company man

Remember, there is no God but Mammon and the company is his profit. Everything which you possess is due to the company's benevolence and all your ambitions, hopes, and aspirations cannot be fulfilled unless you continue to enjoy its favours. Equipped with such attitudes, you will quickly stand out from those who are less committed. Above all you cannot afford to dissipate your energies in time consuming outside interests, however stimulating and rewarding they may often be. There will be plenty of time for such trivialities when you have attained your goals: until then you must concentrate upon the task in hand.

In practical terms, this means that you must be willing to meet every demand which is made upon you, especially those which occur after normal working hours. For example, unless stricken by some contagious disease, you should never fail to attend a major corporate function such as the Christmas Dance; nor should you ever miss a company-sponsored outing to the theatre (no matter how recently you may have seen the play). Similarly, if you are suddenly called upon by your boss to meet an important client, who is arriving at Heathrow at 10 p.m., you will accept with enthusiasm—even if it means cancelling your annual pilgrimage to Covent Garden. After all, it is in such testing fires that future top executives are forged.

However, do not fall into the habit of staying late at the office in the belief that this will prove how dedicated you are. On the contrary, it is far more likely to be taken as evidence of poor organization and of a failure to delegate. Nevertheless, there is much to be said for putting in the occasional Saturday morning stint at the office, especially if you get wind that one or two of the directors will be coming in too. The reason for this is simple. So sacred is the Saturday morning golf match to such men that it will be assumed that anyone not playing must be exceptionally committed.

Cultivate the social graces

You do not need to be a master of etiquette to succeed in business but it will certainly help if you can handle yourself competently at company functions. This does not mean that you should attempt to be a social lion since this may only excite the envy of those less extrovert—a dangerous situation if they are senior to you.

Once again, try to project the right sort of image: modest and cheerful, tactful and sympathetic, the kind of man who never tries to upstage anyone. If ladies are present, you have a gilt edged opportunity to prove that you are one of nature's gentlemen and by practising those small courtesies which, *pace* Women's Lib, are still very much appreciated, you can pile up credits in the boudoir as well as in the boardroom.

It is important too that you learn how to mask your real feelings, even under the most trying circumstances. If the chairman decides to make you the butt of his elephantine wit, so be it. If your boss requires you to be his 'straight man' while he blunders through a succession of ghastly anecdotes, make certain that no one laughs louder than you. But no matter how tempting the prospect or severe the provocation, never be drawn into flirting with another man's wife—there is no surer way of making an enemy for life. When temptation strikes, think not of England but of the company and of how much you both need each other. Alternatively, you can adopt a policy of positive disengagement and, with a murmured excuse, head for the nearest cloakroom. It will only take a few moments for the storm to pass.

You must also remain alert to the numerous other pitfalls which surround such occasions. For example, should you find yourself sitting next to the managing director at dinner, always let him make the conversational running; never show off your knowledge of a subject which he knows nothing about. Ask him questions only if you are sure that he knows the answers and if he has a favourite hobby horse then get him safely mounted on it as quickly as possible. From then on all will be plain sailing: you need only keep nodding at ten second intervals. The chances are that he will remember you afterwards as a bright young man and a most interesting conversationalist, one who knew how to listen as well as talk.

Learn to take criticism

On your way to the summit, there will be many occasions when your actions will be criticized and your judgement questioned. The most difficult situation to contend with is when you believe that you were right, even though things have turned out badly. This, however, is a foolish attitude since it contravenes the first law of business management: whatever succeeds is right and whatever fails requires a scapegoat to be found. And if it should happen to be your turn to be the scapegoat, accept your fate stoically. Remember, it is you who could be using the thumbscrews next week.

Many companies have introduced 'performance appraisal' schemes by which managers review the performance of their immediate subordinates and hand down their verdicts at formal interviews. Such occasions can provide a searching test of your executive calibre since as the prisoner in the dock you are not expected to argue with the judge. Your best strategy is to acknowledge your shortcomings with as good a grace as possible and thank your boss profusely for pointing them out. This is known in business as 'behaving maturely' and will have a most beneficent effect upon your salary progression.

Similarly, if you make a mistake in your work which is not too serious, there is much to be said for confessing it before it is officially detected. To expose yourself willingly to your boss's criticism is a subtle form of flattery since it shows that you are confident of receiving fair treatment. And since it is also considered un-British to kick a man when he is down, it is unlikely that your action will have any serious repercussions (NB this technique is *not* recommended if your boss is an American).

These then are some of the tried and tested ploys which lead directly to the top. If practised assiduously, they will more than compensate for any lack of talent. Indeed, it is surprising that they are not taught in our business schools since, unless you can propel yourself into a management position, what is the point of learning how to manage? Planning, like charity, begins at home, so why not start now to plan for success? It will be a long, hard road but the rewards are great and you have nothing to lose except your self-respect.

8.

The Midas machines

The business of America is business

Calvin Coolidge

Whether we like it or not (and many of us do not) American companies have the general reputation of being markedly more dynamic than their British counterparts. Fired by an almost messianic zeal for profitability and growth, the US multinationals are the modern equivalent of Caesar's legions, arrogant yet irresistible as they continue to plant their standards in the very citadels of their foes. The question is: what makes them tick? Have they some magic success formula which eludes their indigenous competitors? Are their managers more intelligent, better selected, more rigorously trained? Do they attract a special breed of executive, increasingly rare in our large corporations, who thrives upon pressure and actually enjoys taking risks? Dammit, are they just plain *better* than us?

Fear not, O guilt stricken British executive—Armageddon, Detroit-style, is not yet at hand. The downfall of the conglomerates, the off-shore funds fiascos, the lurchings at Lockheed, the indescribable chaos of Penn Railroad—are not these the works of men just as vulnerable as ourselves? Surely no one who has seen executive-type American tourists being effortlessly fleeced by semi-literate vendors in London's West End can still believe in the invincibility of the US businessman? These be ordinary human beings, not a conquering herrenvolk.

And yet, if their human raw material is no more talented than ours, how come that US companies seem to make better use of it? Does the secret lic in the training and development which their managers receive? Are their executives so used to winning mock battles in the classroom that winning the real thing is a foregone conclusion? Here are the techniques which are commonly used to shape potential executives into the corporate mould.

Do-it-yourself

Technically known as 'on the job development', this is the managerial equivalent of natural selection. No technique could be simpler to operate: you merely throw 'em in at the deep end and see who can swim. If the man survives then you nurture and encourage him; if he goes under you advise him to seek his fortune elsewhere. This weeding out process generally takes place during the first year of employment, thus neatly separating the wheat from the chaff.

Apart from short 'orientation' and product courses, it is rare for a man to be exposed to any advanced formal training until he has successfully completed this ordeal by combat. In this way the company saves both the time and the expense involved in backing potential losers since it is an article of faith that the fittest will always survive. Historically, of course, this is a throwback to the old frontiersman tradition when a man survived by his quickness on the draw, but in business terms too it should not be lightly dismissed. After all there are still too many indigenous organizations in which it is the time servers rather than the talented who reach senior positions, their weaknesses glossed over by too indulgent superiors. Happily, such companies are becoming fewer every year as they struggle to meet the challenge of rising costs. Even so, who can deny that there are still some large UK firms in which the entrepreneurial spirit is an emaciated tiger with scarcely enough strength to pad around its cage?

And so for your first year in an American company you are very much on trial, your strengths and weaknesses carefully noted and assessed. There is no mollycoddling whatever. You are expected to ask questions, find things out for yourself, and be willing to assimilate the corporate culture. At the end of it all you are classified as either a man with potential or as one who is unlikely to make the grade. Either way you are left in no doubt where you stand.

Vaccination

The only games which you play in an American company are business games, and you always play to win. Having survived your initial lonely ordeal, you will now be received into the bosom of the company and be required to attend your quota of in-company training courses.

Like everything else in the organization, management training is hard nosed, practical, and geared to results. There is no swanning around with erudite philosophies: everything which is taught must be capable of being implemented. While the potential executive is encouraged to express himself, there is none of the donnish atmosphere of the typical British management course. The course members are serious minded, committed, and invariably enthusiastic. As for the tutors, they often sound like salesmen who are doing their best to disguise the fact that they have university degrees.

The keynote of these courses is tough, hard hitting discussion: no quarter is either given or expected. If the trainer has a weakness, be sure that the course members will find it and exploit it and woe betide the man who cannot illustrate his material with plenty of concrete examples drawn from his personal experience. It is this overwhelming emphasis upon relevance and practicality which make so many American companies in the UK reluctant to give more generous support to some of those pukka British training institutions which, rightly or wrongly, are felt to be mere ivory towers, staffed by men who have opted out of the pressures of day-to-day management. Similarly, many a well known management 'expert' has met his Waterloo when appearing as a guest speaker at in-company management conferences. Accustomed to the gentler and more restrained atmosphere of the British management 'seminar', many are shaken, if not appalled, by the frankness of the questions which are fired at them and by the relentless probing of any answers which are considered to be woolly or vague.

In short, management training courses in US multinationals tend to produce tough, hard headed executives rather than cultivated management theorists. There is, of course, an important spinoff from all this—an unspoken philosophy which affects relationships at all levels within the organization as well as with the unions and other outside bodies. Perhaps this outlook can best be described as one of 'opportunistic pragmatism', a feeling that results alone count and to hell with policies if they stand in the way. It is no accident that the word which is most frequently used by executives in American companies is 'flexibility', which is merely another way of saying 'let's keep our options open'.

The package deal

Tough and empirical though they may be, many American companies are amazingly vulnerable to management gimmicks and panaceas, especially if they come gift wrapped in all the latest psychological jargon. There seems to be a particularly strong appetite for courses which claim to be able to transform an executive's 'management style' or to smooth off the rough edges in his personality. Some cynics have suggested that the susceptibility of American companies to these packages is a direct reflection of their sales orientation, for who is easier to sell to than an experienced salesman? This, however, is only part of the story. The fact is that most American organizations are at heart profoundly optimistic: they see no reason why people should be unwilling to change if only the message which they are given is sufficiently inspirational. Thus, they tend to be impatient with those who counsel caution and who point out the many complex factors which can inhibit change. Characteristically, such companies are interested in quick results: *ergo*, anyone who promises them can be sure of a sympathetic hearing.

Nevertheless, despite operating in such fertile soil, the history of these training packages in American companies is far from being a runaway success story. The reason for this is simple: lack of top management involvement. It is just not realistic to bombard middle and junior management with the latest behavioural science theories and expect them to change when the Board continues to function as a rock ribbed autocracy. It is the old, old story of 'do as I say, not as I do', a situation which has given the death blow to many well intentioned projects (and not only, of course, in American companies).

Surprisingly, however, hope seems to spring eternal in transatlantic breasts. Even though last year's wonder drug may have disappeared without trace, there is always the chance that this year's panacea may turn out to be the magic elixir which will enable the organization to outdistance its competitors. And so once again the treasure chest is opened and high priced executives are made to jump through expensive training hoops. It may be magnificent but surely it is not businesslike?

Esprit de corps

The training which a potential executive receives in an American company is not simply confined to attending formal courses. The organization moves in many mysterious ways, all of which are aimed at producing loyal corporate citizens. The entire resources of a sophisticated multinational public relations machine are brought to bear so that an Englishman working in London soon begins to feel that he has more in common with his opposite number in say, Paris, than with his next door neighbour who works in the City.

And so indeed he has. Little by little he becomes not just a 'UK subsidiary man' but a legionnaire in a vast international army of executives for whom a visit to the States is as commonplace as a Saturday morning shopping trip to the local supermarket. And lest he should begin to develop any 'little Englander' ideas he is reminded at regular intervals of the more spectacular achievements of the great worldwide family of which he is a member. Nearly all US multinationals produce their own monthly newspapers which are circulated to even the most far flung outposts of the corporate empire. Packed with news about exciting new products and outstanding sales triumphs, these international newspapers constantly project the image of the company as an irresistible force, capable of surmounting virtually any obstacle. Nothing detrimental to the corporation is ever printed in these pages; if any battles have been lost they remain unrecorded. From time to time, as a kind of papal benediction, a message from the Chairman is printed in full. The theme of these bulletins is always the same: 'You're doing just great, fellas, but try to keep down those costs'.

There are, of course, a number of tribal rituals which are meticulously observed in each subsidiary. A typical UK example is the annual management conference when the entire management staff, from those in the Jaguar class to drivers of humble Escorts and Avengers, are gathered together for an extended pep talk from top management.

The atmosphere at these meetings is a combination of revivalist meeting and rugby club dinner. General platform speakers are subjected to good natured heckling from an exuberant audience; the latest company newsreels are shown amid irreverent interjections; and there is always a particularly sardonic cheer when the financial director rises to speak. However, once the magic word 'profit' is uttered, a cathedral-like hush falls over the meeting. Even in American companies there are some things which are much too sacred to joke about.

Follow me, men

The great majority of US multinationals were founded by men whose business acumen was equalled only by the strength of their characters and personalities. This belief in the quasi-magical properties of the hard driving leader continues to permeate such organizations today, hence the emphasis which is placed upon man management and leadership training.

Managers in American organizations are under no illusions regarding the importance which the company attaches to the development of subordinates. How a manager chooses to discharge his responsibility is basically up to him. He can be a father confessor or a table-pounding autocrat, a genial colleague or an ice cold bureaucrat. The question is: 'Does he generate sufficient managerial talent within his group?' And, make no mistake, this is a policy which has teeth; many an executive has been passed over for promotion because of his failure to train a competent successor. Given this kind of incentive, no manager with ambition needs to be carried kicking and screaming into the company's management training centre (a situation which, unhappily, is by no means unknown in many British companies). He knows full well that such opportunities are not lightly offered and that there are many other executives who will be only too eager to snap up his place.

The leadership role of the individual manager is therefore of supreme importance in American companies and it is common for a manager's personal style to be duplicated at all levels within his department. Naturally, this 'follow your leader syndrome' quite frequently spills over into areas such as dress and speech. For example, if the executive's language is littered with profanities his subordinates will soon begin using his favourite oaths; if he suddenly displays a penchant for short haircuts and jazzy shirts then his department will quickly abound with crew cutted managers arrayed as colourfully as peacocks. Indeed, in such matters of personal taste, as in so many other areas, an American company is no place for anyone with rigid convictions. To err may be human but to be inflexible is disastrous.

Crystal ball

No executive who works for a US multinational can reasonably complain that he is a forgotten man: there are far too many pairs of eyes observing his performance. First, there is his boss who formally appraises him at least once a year. Then there is the ever-watchful personnel department in which his chief scrutineers will be the personnel manager and the quaintly styled 'manpower resources manager'. Finally, operating at long distance, like a lonely and sometimes malevolent godfather, is the vice president employee relations, into whose hands all reports on executives eventually fall.

Given such a plethora of data, it would be pleasant to report that the plum executive jobs invariably go to the candidates with the best track records. Alas, not so: merit, like patriotism, is not always enough (though it is rare for a blatant mountebank to be appointed). It would, of course, be naive to ignore the influence of political factors in virtually all senior appointments in any large corporation, whether the head office is located in Dallas or in Frinton-on-Sea. But in American companies there is often a particularly subtle form of infighting which makes the British 'old boy net' look like a branch of the Samaritans. No matter how good your performance may be, God help you if you fall foul of your boss (unless, of course, you have powerful connections in the higher echelons of the company or, better still, in politics or the media).

The tragedy of many large American companies is that in spite of having sophisticated 'talent spotting' systems they frequently fail to use them properly; in practice it is the immediate boss who has the last word. Thus, many a talented high flyer has been driven out of a company because his boss regarded him as a dangerous rival and did everything within his power to 'poison the well'. The basically auto-cratic nature of such corporations, the belief that management at any level has the right both to propose and dispose, makes it immensely difficult for any executive who feels that he is being unjustly treated to obtain the support of higher authority, however well founded his complaint may be. Thus, the only way such a man can survive is by playing politics himself and forming alliances, preferably both inside and outside the company. Once he has acquired such protection, it is unlikely that he will be seriously troubled since American companies are particularly sensitive to direct personal confrontations—after all, they destroy the much prized corporate image of 'togetherness' and 'teamwork'.

Thus, despite the abundance of crystal balls—performance appraisals, confidential reports, succession plans, etc.—many executives remain understandably cynical about the extent of their influence and work assiduously to keep their political fences in good repair. And who can blame them?

Nevertheless, American companies have one major psychological 'plus factor' compared with most of their British rivals: their 'classless-ness'. There are far fewer of those carefully drawn boundaries between different levels of employees which still disfigure and inflame relation-ships in so many British companies: the separate restaurants, the executive car parks, the 'staff only' entrance *et al*. It is a commonplace event in an American UK subsidiary to find the managing director standing in line in the self-service restaurant behind a gaggle of secre-taries who may well have joined the company only that morning. A small point perhaps but one which, like the almost universal use of

Christian names, is indicative of that overtly democratic ambience which most American companies strive to create and maintain.

Despite the unfavourable publicity resulting from a few well known trouble spots, there is no doubt that very many UK employees of US multinationals, whatever their status, find such an atmosphere both refreshing and liberating, and it pays off in their performance. The management style may still be paternalistic but at least there are far fewer of those pettifogging, socially divisive practices which provide a built-in source of tension in more hierarchical organizations. This perhaps is the real secret of the American company's success: it has created a society in which there are neither gentlemen nor players. And having deposed class and breeding, it has canonized results.

9.

Horses for courses

Blessed is he who expects nothing
for he shall never be disappointed.

Alexander Pope, Letters, 23 September 1725

When a manager attends an external training course, he faces the challenge of making new relationships, of finding people with whom he can identify. This is especially true of those high priced residential courses where he may find himself incarcerated for several weeks. Happily, within a matter of days, he has usually discovered those whom he finds sympathetic and learned to avoid those who are less agreeable. But whether they prove to be friends or foes, he is certain to meet some of the following types.

The Know-All

Here is a man who considers that he should be running the course, not just attending it. Insulated by his impenetrable ego against almost any new idea, he regards formal training as a waste of time and expresses his views in no uncertain terms. One of his favourite comments is 'that's all right in theory', a sure indication that he is out of his depth.

Seeing himself as a dynamic decision maker, he is an eager contributor to group discussions and quickly becomes noted for his impractical solutions. Paradoxically, his very dimness helps to boost morale since it encourages others to criticize his ideas without ever feeling that he could prove them wrong. Impervious to his role as classroom punchbag, he continues to plug away at his best loved theme: the need for managers to use their 'commonsense'.

Naturally, such a man can play havoc with a tight course schedule. It is not only his irrelevant comments which have to be dealt with: his boring reminiscences must also be stemmed. There is scarcely a topic which does not remind him of some trivial problem in his past career for which, needless to say, he found a brilliant solution. Nor is he diffident about offering his advice to his fellow course members when they air their problems during general discussions. Predictably, such advice is invariably rejected—usually on the grounds that he has missed the point.

Why such men are sent on courses remains a mystery. Perhaps their bosses are out-and-out optimists who are hoping for the equivalent of a miracle at Lourdes? Perhaps they see trainers as powerful alchemists, capable of transforming lead into gold? Or could it be simply that they want a break from the daily ordeal of trying to manage them? One thing is certain: no course is likely to have the slightest effect. Even if the spirit were willing, the brain is too weak.

The Aficionado

This man has generally been on more courses than the rest of the course members put together. Often within a few years of retirement, he is his company's official course evaluator and spends practically all of his time attending conferences and seminars. A veteran of a thousand lectures, he has the air of a man who has seen it all before, like an oil millionaire on a round the world cruise.

He is easily recognized during group discussions by his apparent familiarity with management jargon. This can sometimes mislead his colleagues into regarding him as an expert but such a reputation is invariably shortlived. He is like a seasoned tourist who can parrot a few phrases in several languages but is quite incapable of speaking any of them fluently. In this as in so many other ways he is a perfect example of arrested development.

Nevertheless he is not without a certain cunning and is adept at avoiding any responsible role. For example, he will never volunteer to chair a discussion but will always be the first to nominate someone else. Again, he will modestly decline any attempt to make him a spokesman on the grounds that it is a job for a younger man. During syndicate work he tends to keep a low profile and rarely takes sides if the discussion becomes heated. This is understandable since, having attended dozens of courses, he virtually knows all the arguments by heart.

A true Aficionado is never worried by the pressures of a course. While keen young thrusters work far into the night on complex problems set by the tutors, he sleeps uncaringly after an evening in the bar. After all, he reasons, these are only paper battles and are not worth the effort of staying awake. Far better to get a good night's rest and let all those eager young Turks play at being tycoons.

The Fall Guy
Sending a man on a course is an excellent way of ensuring his absence while his department is reorganized or even abolished (generally speaking, the longer the course the more radical the surgery). Indeed, many an executive has returned from a lengthy course to find that his name has disappeared from the organization chart or that he has lost vital ground in the promotion race.

It is not difficult to perceive why such a man should so often be the victim of internal politicking. He is that archetypal 'nice chap' who is totally incapable of detecting human deviousness and assumes that everyone's motives are as pure as his own. On courses, he finds himself constantly chosen as a chairman or spokesman by men who are only too keen to avoid responsibility and who simply regard him as a malleable innocent. Being ever anxious to please, he accepts their blandishments as a tribute to his ability and willingly performs all the dogsbody jobs.

As a course member he is polite, well mannered, and totally innocuous. He can be relied upon never to lose his temper or to ask an awkward question (even if he thought of one he would never have the courage to ask it). Fearful of any kind of personal confrontation, he quickly back-pedals from the slightest challenge and readily qualifies or even recants any views he has expressed. This is because he believes that togetherness and 'teamwork' are more important than principle: he is the last man you would expect to find manning the barricades.

It is a miracle that such men ever survive in business and indeed many are swept away during takeovers and mergers. Others find themselves shunted into various dead-end jobs where they contentedly await their gold watches and pensions.

The Gadfly
Some executives are only happy when they are criticizing and the Gadfly is perhaps the most obnoxious member of this particular breed. He seems to obtain an almost orgiastic relief from intellectually humiliating his various opponents and figuratively grinding them into the dust. Often a man of considerable mental calibre, he prides himself

upon his command of logic and delights in setting traps for the unwary speaker.

His favourite ploy is to wait for his victim to develop his thesis and then to pounce with an incisive question which purports to expose its apparent 'contradictions'. It is not so much the question which causes his colleagues' hackles to rise as the condescending tone in which it is delivered. Oblivious to the black looks and muffled groans which greet his interventions, he continues to press his point with all the sensitivity of a wounded buffalo, thereby uniting his colleagues in defence of the speaker. However strong his arguments, and sometimes they can be very strong indeed, it is rare for him to obtain any general support since his manner generates such hearty dislike. Thus, he is forced into the role of 'perpetual loner' and hardly ever mixes with the other course members.

It is a pity that his talents should run to waste since he is undoubtedly capable of making a powerful contribution. But on management courses, as in his real life job, his total lack of political skills means that every man's hand is against him as soon as he opens his mouth. While every function is capable of producing its Gadflies, many of them have an accountancy background. The very virtues which make them technically competent, analytical ability and an eye for absurdities, are precisely those which make them unpopular with their colleagues. So often they lack the magic gift of salesmanship: when they have it they can be formidable indeed.

The Scribe

This earnest seeker after truth accumulates knowledge like a miser hoards money. He is far and away the hardest working member of any course and rarely asks questions since he is so busy taking notes. Why he should go to such lengths is curious indeed since very few lecturers have anything new to say (and those who have often find it difficult to communicate). But for the Scribe everything is important and not a point must be lost. In a matter of days he generates enough notes for a full length novel.

Basically he is a rather insecure man who nurtures feelings of guilt about being on the course. He has a compulsive need to prove that he is working hard and regards his notes as a form of evidence. Even when the lecturers provide copious handouts, it has little effect upon his productivity: he continues to beaver away like a budding Tolstoy.

Naturally he has to endure a good deal of banter from his less industrious colleagues and is often given such nicknames as 'Prof' or 'Brains'.

In fact, he is very far from being academically inclined and is virtually bereft of any critical faculty. While his more worldly colleagues frolic in the bar he sits in his room trying to digest his notes or working far into the night on the evening's homework. The result is that he is perpetually tired and takes little part in classroom discussions.

When he returns from the course he produces a voluminous report which contains a blow-by-blow description of each day's work. Needless to say, it is almost never read and is quickly consigned to the obscurity of a file. For both the Scribe and his boss the party is over. It is time to return to more serious things.

The Hearty

For this man going on a course is simply an extension of his annual holiday. He has not the slightest intention of doing any work: he intends to eat well, drink well, and play as much golf as possible. He is nearly always to be found on the 'country house' type of course where the cuisine is excellent and the wines are superb. He tends to avoid courses which are run in West End hotels or in ancient universities with draughty lecture rooms.

With his bucolic countenance and rumbling laugh, he is the Champagne Charlie of any course and is worth his weight in gold for his effect upon morale. Not even the dreariest speaker can daunt his good humour and he has a healthy disrespect for 'scientific management'. For him there is no problem which cannot be solved at the nineteenth hole. He believes that all trade union leaders should be compelled to play golf.

Being essentially a simple soul, he has scant regard for Know-Alls and Gadflies whom he is apt to describe as 'a pain in the arse'. While he is careful not to engage in intellectual swordplay, his no-nonsense personality and cheerful profanity make him a formidable opponent and a powerful ally. He gets on famously with the Aficionado and is often quick to defend the hapless Fall Guy. But being the least self-important of men, he is always ready to joke at his own expense.

The Hearty is most frequently found on those lengthy, easy paced management courses which are favoured by blue chip British companies (and avoided like the plague by US multinationals). Here, amid the Georgian windows and Adam fireplaces, the Hearty is in his element (not that he is interested in cultural matters—it is simply that such an ambience suits his personality). Unhappily, he is a member of a dying race as more and more companies plump for cost effectiveness and begin to squeeze out their management Falstaffs. When the axe falls, Hearties often find jobs as Bursars or Stewards in management colleges where they generally do an excellent job.

The Huckster

So far as this man is concerned he is attending the course for one purpose only—to sell his company's product or service to the other course members. He invariably makes his mark during the opening session when members introduce themselves to their fellow trainees. But whereas most executives confine themselves to a few brief comments, the Huckster launches into an extended commercial, glorifying his company and the product it sells. Cases have been known where Hucksters have actually produced their products and passed them around the table for individual inspection. This does not, of course, apply to those who sell capital goods.

From then on he never lets up and seizes every possible opportunity to brainwash his colleagues. Naturally, most of the really hard selling goes on in the bar but working sessions, too, are not immune from his zeal. He is particularly adept at quoting examples during group discussions which somehow always redound to the benefit of his company. Similarly, when other course members talk about their problems, he is quick to point out that such difficulties could not exist were only his own beloved company involved. This sometimes produces cynical guffaws from those who have dealt with his firm in the recent past.

But for all his constant importuning, the Huckster is usually an extremely pleasant chap and is generous to a fault, a trait which is reflected in his expense accounts. He is one of nature's enthusiasts, a rare breed in management, and is regarded with tolerant amusement by his more phlegmatic colleagues. He honestly believes that he works for the world's finest company which sells the world's finest products. The surprising thing is that he changes his job so frequently; one wonders what it is that makes him so easily disenchanted (could it be the shock of receiving a customer's complaint?).

There are sometimes a number of other characters on management courses who do not turn up as frequently as those who have been dealt with. For example, there is the Toady, who believes that a report on his performance will be sent back to his company and therefore does everything within his power to curry favour with the lecturers. Then there is the Truant, a man who is constantly stricken by a number of minor ailments which result in him missing numerous working sessions, particularly those which involve him in chairing discussions. Not least, there is the Fanatic, a man who nurses a pet hate—it could be shop stewards, pop music, or any number of things—and who suddenly launches into a vehement diatribe which paralyses discussion until the storm has passed.

As for the lecturers, they learn to ride with the punches and quickly develop a protective shell. After all, to leave one's emotions exposed is simply to invite a breakdown: survival demands a far more clinical approach. And if such courses did not exist, then what would companies *do* with all their problem managers? Not even hospitals can provide this kind of therapy.

10.

How to sack a boss

Sack the lot!

Lord Fisher, Letter to *The Times*, 2 September 1919

Generally speaking, firing executives is bad for business. Not only does it generate uncertainty, it invariably results in the company having to pay premium prices on the open market to obtain replacements for those who have left. Even where successors are available within the organization, the new men are likely to perform cautiously rather than with panache. Once the axe has been wielded, memories die hard.

This is not to say that poor performers must never be removed from their jobs: indeed they must, or profits may crumble. Surprisingly, however, some companies seem totally unaware of the many techniques which can be used either to induce a voluntary resignation or to redeploy an executive in a less responsible post. Here are several which have proved their worth.

Moon shot
This is based upon the principle of making the rat race work for you. Since most executives are ambitious, an offer of promotion is difficult to refuse, especially when accompanied by such trappings of success as a larger car, a grander office, and the right to employ a personal assistant.

Moves of this kind do require meticulous planning. First, the new job must be carefully drained of any activities which could affect the company's business results. Next, the appointment must be announced in such a way as to assuage any suspicions on the part of the executive that he is being punished for failure rather than rewarded for success. This is normally achieved by a lyrically worded management circular. Sometimes, to add extra credibility, an action photograph of the promoted executive, showing him working at his desk, is published in the company magazine. Such accolades are, of course, strictly reserved for the more senior, and popular, executives whose removal, if unexplained, might pose a threat to morale.

Ego trip
Never underestimate the power of the human ego: rare indeed is the executive who can resist the role of company guru, however infrequently his advice may be heeded.

Many a failed executive has wept with joy upon being channelled into some notorious company backwater, having been given a title such as 'internal consultant' or 'group coordinator'. The fact that no one consults him or that he has nothing to coordinate is, for him, irrelevant: the important thing is that the company has recognized his statesmanship and capacity for dispensing objective advice. One senior personnel manager who, having been directly responsible for a disastrous strike had been appointed 'group labour relations consultant', told me that he regarded himself as 'the conscience of the company'. Such men have an infinite capacity for self-delusion and, given the opportunity, will literally sprint into corporate oblivion. Responsibility, like beauty, is in the eye of the beholder.

Course roulette
Carry out the following experiment. Each time one of your subordinates attends an external training course, ask him to let you have a copy of the list of course members. At the end of a year, scrutinize these lists and write down any names which appear more than four times.

These people are the Corporate Bedouins, the managerial counterparts of the nomads of Arabia. Assigned by their companies to evaluate new methods and techniques (their reports are usually filed, unread), they move from course to course, trailing clouds of amiable bewilderment and dutifully asking the same two or three questions. They represent a kind of hard core underemployed, condemned to a life of perpetual studentship amid the comfortable trappings of three star hotels.

They are rarely in their offices long enough to obstruct any changes which are initiated during their absence. However, when a major reorganization is imminent, such men are often sent into temporary exile at one of the European business schools. Since their jobs have usually undergone radical surgery by the time they return, they tend to encounter above-average frustration in applying what they have learned.

White man's grave

The giant international companies have long been accustomed to using their overseas subsidiaries for the occasional export of surplus executives. Indeed, in some companies the international division is regarded as a kind of penal battalion for recalcitrants from the home operation.

However, provided that the organization is geographically dispersed, it is not necessary to have overseas interests in order to apply this technique: an office in Cleethorpes will do just as well as a refinery in Sarawak. Given the cooperation of a well trained secretary who can be relied upon to mislay all communications emanating from the exiled executive, with the exception, of course, of his letter of resignation, there is no reason at all why he should ever resurface.

Happily, most of these remittance men eventually go native and become respected figures in their local communities.

Deep Freeze

Most executives seek to establish friendly relationships with their superiors and colleagues: such contacts form part of the 'psychic income' of their jobs. Deprive an executive of these human satisfactions and invariably his performance will suffer.

Deep Freeze is a technique which tends to have an accumulative rather than an immediate effect upon the executive concerned. It may begin with the omission of his name, seemingly by accident, from general management circulars and memoranda. Gradually, the tempo quickens. Meetings which he would normally be invited to attend are held in his absence; he begins to find it difficult to gain access to his superior; conversation flags when he joins his colleagues for lunch; his subordinates appear embarrassed and ill at ease; his superior's secretary becomes distinctly offhand.

The crunch comes quickly, usually about the time when he is expecting a salary review. Now, in the judicial atmosphere of an 'appraisal interview', he learns that he is lacking in initiative, in drive, in creativity, and in leadership—indeed, that he is lucky to have been kept on the payroll during the past 23 years. He may care, it is suggested, to look for alternative employment.

Pressure cooker

This technique is often used to ease out middle ranking executives who seem unlikely to cope with the growth of their jobs. Under the guise of delegating more responsibility in order to develop his subordinate, the superior unleashes a veritable blizzard of new assignments for completion in addition to the man's normal duties. At the same time, a number of new control procedures are introduced, resulting in a substantial increase in both the volume and length of his written reports.

Should the executive succeed in weathering this onslaught, there are other ploys which can be used, all with the pretext of broadening his experience. He can be rotated into a number of jobs, none of which hold the slightest appeal for him, in other departments or locations; he can be required to take part in lengthy 'potential assessment procedures', involving rigorous psychological testing and protracted sessions with the company psychiatrist; or he can be assigned for special coaching to one or more executives with whom he is known to be on unfriendly terms.

While he is away being developed, his job is, of course, filled, and on his return he has little choice but to accept the offer of a sideways move.

One final *caveat*. There is one man in every organization upon whom none of these techniques will have any effect, the managing director. Removing him requires ammunition of a far heavier calibre and a special kind of marksmanship that is extremely rare. Ambitious executives, however, need not despair for under every MD's chair lurks an ever-present time bomb: profit responsibility.

Envy not his Bentley, nor his liveried chauffeur. When you are that far up you can only go down.

11.

Back to the jungle

I think I could turn and live with animals,
they are so placid and self-contain'd.

Walt Whitman, *Song of Myself*

In many articles and discussions on business, executives are portrayed as being engaged in a 'rat race' or as predators roaming 'the executive jungle'. Time and again we are told that success is a question of 'the survival of the fittest' and that those who succeed 'claw' their way to the top. Regardless of whether such comments are justified, there are indeed some remarkable similarities between life in the jungle and the world of business. Here are examples of animal behaviour patterns which are by no means unknown in the executive suite.

The lion

Unquestionably the most regal of beasts, the lion is the jungle's dynamic MD. When he roars the whole forest trembles and even the more powerful predators lie low in their lairs. At times like these he will attack almost any animal, particularly the more slow witted beasts who have not yet sensed his dangerous mood.

It is not known for certain what causes these rages. Some say that he suffers from chronic indigestion, others that he is driven by a power complex. Judging by the behaviour of his human counterpart it is more likely that it is a mixture of both.

Outside the lion's den lies his faithful mate. Her job, like that of the MD's secretary, is to ward off visitors who may be unwelcome and to preserve the sanctity of his afternoon nap. Although she may sometimes appear a little long in the tooth, she is none the less a formidable adversary with her razor-sharp claws and harsh, rasping tongue.

Sad to relate, as she nears old age, she is often supplanted by a younger lioness who at first may be more tolerant of the lesser breeds. But as time passes she reverts to type and becomes just as imperious as her predecessor.

The gorilla

A gorilla on the rampage is like an angry sales manager. Eyes blazing, nostrils flared, he grinds his teeth when particularly frustrated and pounds his chest to emphasize his authority. For such a bulky animal he moves surprisingly quickly, scorning the official jungle paths and preferring to crash through the surrounding foliage.

When not enraged by other animals, he can be playful, good natured, and extremely gregarious. He likes to sport with his fellow gorillas and sometimes these revels last far into the night. Judging by the uproar, they enjoy themselves immensely though more sensitive creatures find it difficult to sleep.

Despite his forbidding outward appearance, the gorilla is not nearly as ferocious as he at first appears. He is an excellent, if authoritarian, husband and father and can be amazingly gentle for such a powerful beast. He is a hearty eater and will often roam far afield in search of food. Sometimes he may be absent for several days but will generally bring back titbits for his mate and offspring. It may be that these are a kind of peace offering since while he is away they must fend for themselves.

Just as many sales managers enjoy swinging a golf club, so the gorilla enjoys swinging from tree to tree. There is no evidence that this has any competitive significance but it would appear to have a calming effect.

The chimpanzee

With his incessant chattering and love of the limelight, the chimp is the jungle's PRO, ever ready to show off his amusing tricks and easily identified by his high pitched screech. During daylight hours he climbs unceasingly and even after dark he is sometimes active. But despite his noise he is a peaceful animal who dislikes confrontations of any kind.

Like the PRO he loves to be noticed and can become somewhat

tetchy if he is continually ignored. His habit of jumping up and down to attract attention is usually a sign of growing impatience, especially if accompanied by a surly scowl. Fortunately, it is rare for such tantrums to last very long and he is soon his old clownish self again. This is just as well, for as every PRO knows it is all too easy to ruin an image.

Through his ability to perform certain human functions, the chimp is regarded as highly intelligent but there is evidence which suggests that he has been overrated. Certainly, he is an excellent zoological showman and knows how to play upon an audience's emotions. But one cannot help wondering whether his perennial cheerfulness is not at times just a little bit forced. After all, as with some human beings, an ear-splitting grin is no proof of good nature. It can just as easily mask a vacant mind.

The rhino
Short sighted and even more short tempered, the rhino is like a hard pressed production manager. He communicates through a series of short, sharp grunts which smaller animals find extremely intimidating, though it is doubtful whether he means them any real harm.

Though naturally cumbersome, he can move like lightning when the need arises and once he breaks into a shambling trot only the most foolhardy animal will stand in his way. Like an irate works manager a charging rhino is virtually unstoppable and it is best to take cover while these brainstorms last. Snorting with rage, he will crash through almost any obstacle but having a tough hide and little imagination it is unlikely that he feels any pain at all.

The rhino compensates for his myopia by his acute sense of hearing and continually picks up messages on the jungle telegraph. These can sometimes cause him to behave irrationally and occasionally to fly into unnecessary panics. Being inherently suspicious of other animals, he leads a somewhat lonely existence and prefers the company of his fellow rhinos. They are the only creatures he seems able to stand.

The vulture
With his sharp eye for detail and lugubrious manner, the vulture is the accountant of the animal world. Being naturally attracted to other animals' misfortunes, he is never far away when tragedy occurs, despite his tendency to hover in the background until it is clear that all hope has been lost.

Like the accountant, the vulture has a profound distaste for any form of waste, though his method of dealing with it is somewhat extreme.

Likewise, he has the accountant's ability to sense impending disaster and can spot even the most trivial discrepancies in an animal's behaviour. Once he swoops down upon his lifeless prey, other vultures follow suit and gather from miles away to share in the feast.

Nevertheless, despite his sinister appearance and lack of charm, the vulture performs a vital function in keeping the jungle reasonably clean. Indeed, were it not for his waste recycling activities many more animals would succumb to disease. Like the accountant's, his is a thankless task and he is invariably unpopular with the other animals. He bears all this with his usual fortitude, apart from an occasional outraged squawk.

The giraffe

In many large concerns there are men of stature whose job it is to peer into the future. In human organizations they are known as corporate planners: their animal counterpart is the lofty giraffe.

The giraffe is a shy, somewhat insular beast who likes to stand aloof from the common herd. Being naturally of a quiet disposition, he tends to avoid the noisier extroverts, particularly the ever-babbling chimp and the powerful gorilla with his deep throated roar. As he gazes dreamily into the distance he could almost be trying to detect the future—alas, with no more success than most corporate planners.

When danger threatens, either real or imagined, he is galvanized into speedy action and is amazingly agile for so ungainly a beast. Unhappily, his warnings are often ignored by the other animals who remain grazing peacefully until disaster strikes. Like the corporate planner he spends much of his time with his neck extended, a posture which leaves him dangerously exposed. He is particularly vulnerable to attacks from the lion for whom he is generally easy prey.

The jackal

One of the shrewdest denizens of the animal kingdom, the jackal has much in common with the personnel manager. Lacking the physique of the lion or the gorilla, he is forced to rely upon his native cunning and his unerring instinct for his own best interests.

A swift and silent prowler, there is little in the jungle which escapes his notice. While he will defend himself ferociously if his escape route is blocked, he generally prefers to work by stealth and will rarely attack any animal larger than himself. He is notably deferential towards the lion and has a healthy respect for the elephant too. Realizing that neither can be vanquished in open combat, he concentrates his efforts upon trying to outwit them and often meets with considerable success.

Just as the personnel manager needs to win the confidence of the managing director, so the jackal tries to ingratiate himself with the larger predators. He is not above doing a little scavenging for the lion and bringing back titbits for his master to devour. Some experts believe that he acts as a kind of spy, noting the movements of other animals and keeping his protector fully informed.

The elephant

With his natural dignity and impressive proportions, the elephant is the chairman of the animal world. Even the noble lion must defer to his majesty and for the other beasts he is a kind of father figure, immensely respected if seldom seen.

Like many chairmen, the elephant is very leisurely in his physical movements. He loves to doze during the afternoons and can remain virtually motionless for hours on end, particularly if he has just visited a watering hole. It is unwise to disturb him in this comatose state since he is invariably ill-tempered and crotchety with intruders and will make menacing gestures of anger and dismissal.

Generally, however, the elephant is a placid enough beast—understandably since he has nothing to fear. He has an enormous appetite but, unlike some chairmen, seems totally unaffected by his gargantuan meals. Nevertheless, despite his air of senatorial calm, his intelligence and perceptiveness should never be underestimated. For behind that soporific exterior lies a wide awake brain, as those who take liberties quickly discover.

There is, of course, one major difference between life in the jungle and the executive suite—animals, unlike executives, know their place. No vulture can hope to usurp the lion nor need the elephant fear the giraffe. How different from life in some large corporations where no man is safe from the assassin's dagger and even a clerk may dream of future greatness. But isn't it exciting to have such opportunities? How *can* those animals be so dumb?

12.

Tries hard, could do better

Use every man after his desert and who should 'scape whipping?
Shakespeare, *Hamlet,* Act II, Scene II

As a man struggles to climb the business ladder invariably his performance is closely watched and assessments are made of his strengths and weaknesses. Most companies now operate formal appraisal schemes which provide a record of individual progress and frequently influence promotion decisions. Unfortunately, some of the methods in use are about as accurate as a blunderbuss. Instead of spurring a man on to improve his performance they simply succeed in de-motivating him.

The gut system
Most managers believe themselves to be good judges of people but some seem to think that they have psychic powers. Such men are in their element in the selection interview which provides an ideal forum for their dubious talents. The main thing to remember about these managerial clairvoyants is that their judgements owe nothing to logic or reason. They operate entirely by 'gut reaction' and if your face doesn't fit you are doomed from the start.

No amount of training in the skills of interviewing is likely to have the slightest effect. After all, if you believe that you can assess a man 'as he comes through the door', such newfangled techniques are a waste of time. True, as a 'goodwill gesture', the candidate may be asked a few stereotyped questions, usually about his sporting interests. But no effort will be made to explore his abilities. The die has been cast within the first two minutes.

There is, of course, no consistency whatever in the prejudices of such men. Some believe that red hair is synonymous with bad temper and that men of short stature are bound to be aggressive. Others claim that a feeble handshake denotes lack of character and that close set eyes are a sign of deviousness. Indeed, there is scarcely a human facet, whether physical or verbal, for which some piece of folklore cannot be found. Talking to these men about a candidate's performance is like taking a course in way-out psychiatry, full of wild speculations in place of facts.

Naturally the company suffers. Little by little, whole departments are taken over by men who are carbon copies of their predecessors. Not only do these men look alike and dress alike—they think alike too. The result is that radical new thinking is driven underground and the company begins to falter from lack of ideas. Those few individualists who still remain are soon made aware that they must adapt or perish. 'Sorry, old boy, but you are not our type' has sounded the knell for many a promising executive.

The superman syndrome
One of the most common methods of appraising an executive is to measure him against a set of personality traits, ranging from 'honesty', 'integrity', 'dependability', and 'trustworthiness' to that familiar duo 'initiative' and 'drive'. There is, of course, no objective way of measuring these qualities but this doesn't deter the amateur psychiatrist—he positively revels in 'playing God'.

This search for the ideal 'management profile' has done more to discredit performance appraisal than almost any other single factor. It has provided the jealous superior with a gift wrapped parcel of 'dirty tricks' with which to safeguard himself against brighter subordinates. For example, by deliberately overloading a 'high flyer' with work he can virtually ensure that the man will fail. He can then report on his 'lack of drive' and express similar reservations about his readiness for promotion.

Another grave drawback of this type of system is that it is impossible to apply any common standards. A man can be rated as 'stubborn' or 'determined' depending upon whether he is liked; one assessor's meat can be another's poison. No wonder that these practices have endured for so long: they give enormous power to those who use them. It is like administering laws which have never been defined—the risk of being challenged is virtually nil.

Personality centred appraisal systems have more in common with schoolboy fantasies than with serious attempts to measure performance. They are a throwback to the world of Superman, that intrepid hero with all the talents. Certainly, if they were taken seriously, they would require executives to behave like saints. But fortunately there is usually a happy ending; they sink under the weight of their own absurdity.

Play school

One of the more bizarre appraisal techniques is 'group selection' whereby men who are thought to have management potential participate in a number of practical exercises under the critical gaze of a panel of executives. Cribbed by industry from the Higher Civil Service, the method puts a premium upon communications skills, especially the ability to speak in public. The strong silent type is at a grave disadvantage whereas the skilful politician can hardly fail to shine.

The pattern of these meetings is invariably the same. First, there are the paper-and-pencil tests which are designed to explore an individual's psyche and to illuminate any unusual quirks. Despite the protests of company psychologists, there can be little doubt that the real purpose of these tests is to weed out the mavericks, and indeed any who do not fit the corporate mould. Next comes the 'leaderless group' exercise—a free-for-all discussion on a controversial topic which the members are expected to run by themselves. Here the recipe for success is simple but effective: always volunteer to take the chair. Such an act is thought to demonstrate initiative and be an infallible sign of 'leadership potential'.

After lunch each participant gives a short talk on a topic assigned to him by the programme director. While this can be an ordeal for the taciturn individual, it is manna from heaven for the uninhibited extrovert. This is where all those public speaking course tricks can really pay off: the firm direct gaze, the pregnant pause, and above all the emotive peroration which evokes an outbreak of spontaneous applause. Finally, there is the 'in-tray' exercise which tests the individual's sense of priorities by requiring him to take action on a mass of paperwork. The main thing to remember about this particular task is to give top priority to mail from the boss. This shows that you recognize who 'calls the shots' and have a proper deference for higher authority.

This 'play school' approach to performance appraisal is still fairly uncommon within the UK, apart from a few multinational companies. In spite of the claims which are made for its effectiveness, it is essentially an exercise in make believe and its predictive value is extremely suspect. It certainly shows who can do the exercises but this is no guarantee of performance on the job itself.

Cloak and dagger

An even more indefensible form of appraisal is that object of mystery, the confidential report. Indeed it is hard to conceive of a better instrument for thoroughly de-motivating senior staff. There is virtually nothing to be said in its favour; it is simply a relic of a bygone era.

Consider the facts. First, under this type of system, the man is rarely allowed to read his report; it may not even be discussed with him. Secondly, even if there is a discussion, he is totally dependent upon his superior's willingness to talk to him frankly about his strengths and weaknesses. Unhappily, many appraisers find it difficult to be forthright and steer well clear of any controversial items which are likely to result in a heated argument. The executive has no way of knowing where he stands and can easily jump to the wrong conclusions.

There are more sinister factors too. It is all too easy for a Machiavellian superior to retard the progress of a man who he dislikes or who he sees as a threat to his own position. Just as 'dead men tell no tales' so there can be no defence against the kind of character assassination which frequently occurs in these secret reports. Many a distorted 'profile' has been drawn through a subtle combination of half truth and malice and many a man has missed promotion as a direct result. Conversely, those who are subservient and pose no threat can be rewarded by an appraisal couched in flattering terms. Either way, the appraiser cannot lose. He is virtually impregnable behind his cloak of secrecy.

But even where such factors do not apply, there is a fatal flaw in most written reporting systems. They assume the presence of a talent which is all too rare in management: the ability to write clear, analytical prose. Many reports are so vague and woolly as to be practically useless for appraisal purposes, reflecting their authors' distaste for such a time-consuming chore. And however much personnel men may deplore this outlook, they would be wise to accept it as a fact of life. The customer, after all, is sometimes right.

Scout's honour

In line with the current emphasis upon employee participation, many firms are encouraging executives to appraise themselves. Instead of merely passively accepting his boss's judgements, the executive is required to review his own performance and to report objectively on his successes and failures. Compared with the injustices of the confidential report, this is a much more refreshing approach to appraisal and is often brought in with the best of intentions. Unfortunately, as so frequently happens, there is sometimes a gulf between theory and practice.

The snag is that you cannot expect autocrats to behave like democrats. If the company climate is still basically authoritarian then self-appraisal will be seen as a meaningless gimmick and its benefits dissipated through fear and distrust. Men who have been used to living in managerial Kremlins cannot be expected to communicate freely simply because their masters appear to have changed their minds; they know that such changes may only be temporary. This is why so many self-appraisal schemes fail to take root: the packaging may be different but what of the product?

Even in more enlightened companies there are still many difficulties to be overcome. The fact is that many executives are embarrassed at having to judge themselves and are naturally wary of being too out-spoken. There is, after all, a fairly thin dividing line between expressing pride in achievement and appearing to brag; conversely, to be absolutely frank about one's personal failures strikes some executives as tantamount to suicide. Who knows but that such things will not be 'used in evidence' at a later date? Every experienced manager knows of such cases; he can hardly be blamed for 'playing it cool'.

Nevertheless, self-appraisal is a step in the right direction. It certainly has a brighter future than the old boss-centred systems and is much more in tune with current trends in society. In any case, it is perhaps no bad thing to ask a manager to look inwards. It is as good a test as any of his emotional maturity.

Hangman's noose

In a perfect world every executive would be judged by his results and all promotions would be made strictly on merit. These are the motivating ideals behind Management By Objectives, now the dominating influence upon executive appraisal. And since such concepts are virtually unarguable and are entirely in tune with our meritocratic age, what possible objections could there be to their use?

The answer is plenty. As many executives have found to their cost, it all depends upon who sets the objectives and whether or not they are realistic. Moreover, unless a man's resources are adequate and he has the necessary authority to act, he can find himself climbing a managerial Eiger where any mistake could be his last. Again, should circumstances change which are beyond his control, are his objectives reset or must he 'press on regardless' in a hopeless attempt to achieve the impossible? No wonder that MBO is sometimes regarded as a 'hangman's noose'; when applied insensitively it can have fearful consequences.

Another common objection to this system is that it generates mountains of paperwork and transforms executives into bureaucrats. Once again, it must be admitted that some disciples of MBO have shown more enthusiasm than common sense by showering managers with voluminous forms which are needlessly complex and take hours to complete. It is the old, old management story of fine tools being ruined by bad workmanship. The failure of MBO systems in many companies is often more of a reflection upon management practice than upon the inherent weaknesses of the system itself.

MBO is now showing signs of entering a new and more mature phase, having survived the traumas of its turbulent adolescence. But make no mistake: it is no panacea and can be misused just as easily as any other technique. Nevertheless, at least it points the way to a better future. With most other systems no future exists.

As might be expected in such a nebulous area, there are a number of other appraisal cults, each with its band of devoted followers. For example, there are those who believe that posture is the key and that a man's character can be judged by the way he sits. Then there are the handwriting experts; the wife vetters; the 'outward bound' enthusiasts; and, most exotic of all, the knife-and-fork brigade for whom a man's table manners reveal his potential. There is indeed no shortage of witch doctors and sorcerers. One can only hope that companies survive their spells.

13.

That boxed-in feeling

Sweet spring, full of sweet days and roses,
A box where sweets compacted lie.

George Herbert, *Virtue*

In every large organization, whether public or private, there is continuous rivalry to win favour and advancement. Backbiting and feuding are not merely occasional phenomena; they are an integral part of Organization Man's life. This is hardly surprising for when people band together for almost any purpose they become in fact a *political* body. A man's influence depends upon his ability to manoeuvre, not simply upon his professional skills.

One of the most searching tests of an executive's ingenuity comes when he finds himself trapped in his current job with very little prospect of moving on. It may be that his function is no longer expanding and that demand for his services is beginning to wane. Worse still, his boss may have reached his ceiling in the company and be blocking promotion for those beneath him. The question is: how can the executive free himself and start his career moving once again? Fortunately, there are a number of useful techniques which can help to break this kind of deadlock.

Divide and conquer
One of the few 'management principles' which industry practises is the

idea that no one should have more than one boss. 'Unity of command' is still a fashionable concept, despite the fact that it is a recipe for stagnation. For to leave your future in the hands of one man is like gambling your savings on a single race; the level of risk is unacceptably high.

The ambitious executive makes no such mistake. He strives constantly to expand his responsibilities so as to increase his visibility with senior management. He is continually on the lookout for assignments and projects which will enable him to leap over functional barriers and meet other executives whom he is keen to impress. Staff executives are particularly well placed to use this technique since they frequently operate across the whole of the company, providing advice and expertise to operating management. This is why so many finance men become senior line managers; they capitalize upon their opportunities to 'sell themselves'.

Frankly, to be connected with only one boss is virtually an announcement of inferior status. The man who has really arrived will be spider-webbed off in several directions by his network of contacts in other departments. But to enter this league you must not only be capable in your specialist field; you must also be prepared to undertake chores. Many an executive has risen to prominence through his ability to solve a relatively trivial problem which has been troubling the chairman for some considerable time. You should work flat out when such opportunities occur since there is no surer way of attracting favourable comment.

Communicate outwards
If you hide your light under a bushel you will never break out; you must constantly work at improving your image. Once again, you must seize every opportunity to get known in the company so that you begin to stand out from the corporate herd. For example, never miss a chance to attend a company conference at which senior managers are likely to be present. Such meetings may be unproductive from the work point of view but they provide a golden opportunity to make yourself known.

Similarly, if you are nominated for an in-company training course, do not plead to be excused because of pressure of work. Instead, be the ideal course member, scrupulously attending each session on time and participating enthusiastically in all the discussions. Whenever the course director calls for a volunteer, be sure to step forward with self-deprecating humility and even if you make an ass of yourself hide your chagrin. Every course director loves a 'trier' and since such men may be consulted in promotion situations it is worth while creating a good impression. Needless to say, never ask a question which is blatantly hostile or display attitudes which could be construed as cynical or indifferent.

Sometimes an executive who is located far away from headquarters may understandably feel handicapped in the promotion race and may develop neurotic feelings of exploitation or neglect. That boxed-in feeling becomes almost a physical reality and he may begin to see himself as a forgotten legionnaire, rotting away in some distant outpost. Such attitudes are as unnecessary as they are self-defeating for there are many things which can be done to reduce the distance factor. For example, the farther you are from corporate HQ the more important it is that you write frequent reports, with copies to other 'interested parties', the executives whom you are trying to impress. Similarly, you will be quick to grasp opportunities to visit headquarters and to manufacture excuses if no real ones exist. And, of course, you will be extra-helpful when head office dignitaries visit your location. Arranging for temporary membership of the local golf club is a ploy which is certain to be well received.

Do some strategic socializing

You have got to have a strategy for moving ahead: companies help those who help themselves. For the boxed-in executive it is a case of 'any port in a storm'; he must extract the maximum benefit from every situation. Such opportunities are not confined to business matters; some of the most fruitful occur outside working hours.

It goes without saying that virtually any company function such as a dance or an outing bristles with opportunities for making valuable contacts. Many top executives like nothing better than to be surrounded by an admiring audience and no one will resent it if you join the circle. Naturally, you must be completely self-effacing and must not try to win the limelight in any way. Your function is simply to act as a corporate flunkey, paying rapt attention to the most boring anecdote and laughing immoderately at the feeblest quip. However, there is nothing to prevent you from asking a few simple questions which will undoubtedly trigger off further reminiscences. The great man will be delighted at such evidence of your interest and may even begin thinking of you as a potential director.

It is surprising that more executives do not attend courses in the social graces since such skills can reap dividends at company functions, particularly with the wives of senior executives. Few things are more flattering to a corporate matriarch than to be attentively courted, albeit platonically, by a well groomed executive with impeccable manners. It is not difficult during such coy encounters to make a casual remark about needing a 'challenge' and how much you admire her husband's work. While you should not expect any dramatic developments, there is every chance that your remarks will be repeated and your name quietly noted as a worthwhile prospect. A word of warning. Do not be crass enough to join the chairman's golf club or to move into a neighbourhood where the MD lives. Such ploys will do nothing to enhance your prospects. You will merely be regarded as a pushy young upstart.

Form tactical alliances
If you are relying upon the company's career development programme to liberate you from your box, you are likely to have to wait for a very long time indeed. Despite all those gaily coloured 'replacement charts' and 'succession tables' only a simpleton puts his trust in such meaningless baubles. They may be the personnel department's pride and joy but they are usually ignored when the decisions are made.

Be smart—forget these trinkets and create your own opportunities. Look around the organization for men who are clearly promotable and do your utmost to establish friendly relationships. In this way you will multiply the power of your eyes and ears so that when vacancies occur you will be forewarned and forearmed. As these friendships blossom, you can express your concern about your prospects and indicate that you would welcome a more challenging role. In other words, subtly but effectively, you can advertise your availability—and without all the fuss of a transfer request.

Of course, should you be fortunate enough to win the friendship of a powerful senior executive, you have a gilt edged opportunity to forge ahead of the pack. However, you should be extremely discreet in the way you conduct the relationship or it may adversely affect your future prospects. To have a secret sponsor is a wonderful thing but if you brag about your friendship the benefits will be 'blown'. Be careful that you are not seen in his office too often and resist the temptation to invite him to lunch. As long as he knows what you are looking for, you must stifle your impatience and bide your time.

Making friends in business is a long term investment and it may be some time before the dividends roll in. Such alliances can, as it were, 'work for you in your sleep' and should be carefully nurtured or they may wither and die. Their main advantage is that they increase your opportunities by opening doors which would otherwise be closed. You cannot expect such help from succession charts; they are the products of bureaucrats, not entrepreneurs.

Build an outside reputation

Plunging into extracurricular activities can be a valuable way of attracting attention, though there are a number of pitfalls for the unwary operator. It is unwise, for example, to become too closely identified with a political party since companies have to deal with all kinds of governments and if you are too partisan you may damage your prospects. The key point to remember about outside activities is that they should benefit the company, not merely yourself.

This still leaves you with plenty of scope. You can work in the evening for a popular charity. Become a governor of a local school. Help to raise money for a new building in your community. Volunteer to help organize a pensioners' outing. All of these activities will reflect favourably upon the company which will be seen as encouraging responsible citizenship. And since many companies are sensitive to their social obligations your praiseworthy efforts are unlikely to be unnoticed.

Writing for trade journals is another useful way of gaining visibility, so long as you do not reveal any secrets to competitors. Such articles can make a valuable contribution to the marketing effort and will be greatly appreciated by senior management. Be careful, however, not to write on more controversial themes which may cause indignant letters to be written to the editor. Cause one major fracas and you could stay boxed-in for life, assuming that you would not be asked to resign.

One possible result of these outside activities is that you may receive an offer from another company. Even if you do not intend to accept, it will give you an excellent opportunity to discuss your future. It is amazing how quickly an offer from a competitor will concentrate attention upon your 'career development'. You can beaver away for years and be taken for granted but let another company bid for your services and you become a priceless member of the management team. But be careful not to overplay your hand. It is absurd to 'point the gun' unless you are prepared to use it.

Create upward pressures

Another way of breaking out of your box is to demonstrate that you are ready for a bigger job. But performance alone is not enough; you need to create the conditions which will permit you to move. For example, never make the mistake of becoming too specialized; you will simply be running a one horse race. And should technical progress make your expertise obsolete, you could well be left with nothing to offer.

So watch out for opportunities to broaden your scope. Talk to executives from other functions and impress them with your willingness to learn. Show interest in their current problems and flatter them with your respectful questions. Above all, remember that there is no surer way of making friends in business than to ask a man to give you some 'candid advice'. If you take his advice he becomes obligated to help you to achieve the results which you are hoping for.

You can also increase your 'mobility potential' by studying for qualifications outside your own field, say for a diploma in marketing if you are a financial man. Be sure, of course, to publicize your efforts by keeping the personnel department informed and by discussing your studies with the relevant company specialists. There is no point in toiling away unnoticed; you must let it be known where your interests lie.

You can also create certain pressures from below by developing competent subordinates who need advancement, a favourite textbook 'solution' to this type of problem. But like most management theories it has its practical drawbacks, not least that the pupil may outdistance his master. It is one thing to develop a man to take your place but quite another to see him jump over your head. However, provided that you are alert to these potential dangers, it should be perfectly possible to have the best of both worlds. After all, unless he too has read this chapter, he is likely to regard you as his all-powerful patron on whose grace and favour he is entirely dependent. It is your job to see that he stays this way by firmly discouraging any delusions of grandeur.

One final point. Should none of these techniques produce results then you would be well advised to seek employment elsewhere. Life is far too short to spend one's years seething and the longer you stay the more frustrated you will get. Moreover, if you delay too long in making your decision you will find yourself so locked in by your company benefits that a move becomes too expensive to contemplate. Don't trade in your talent for a company car. Remember, somewhere out there someone needs you.

14.

Company rituals

Keep up appearances; there lies the test;
The world will give thee credit for the rest.

Charles Churchill, Night

Every organization has its rituals and business is no exception. Just as a church has its high days and feasts to mark the various watersheds in the religious year, so a company has its moments of organized joy and mass celebration. Individuals, too, sometimes band together in more localized rituals which serve to emphasize their identity as a group. These can range from lavish sales conferences in five star hotels to lunchtime drinks in the local pub.

There is no doubt that, regardless of status, most employees enjoy these rituals. After all, they help to break down barriers between departments, enable people to make new friends, and, if only for a few fleeting hours, create a kind of family atmosphere which may be sadly lacking in the workplace itself. But beware; even under the most seemingly carefree conditions there are pitfalls in store for the unwary executive.

The Christmas Dance

This is generally the most spectacular of all company rituals and the supreme event in the social calendar. Attendance is virtually obligatory for all senior executives; any who fail to turn up are looked upon as disloyal shirkers. Indeed, in many companies the fact that an executive misses the Dance is taken as sure-fire proof that he intends to leave. Naturally, this does not apply to those who have suffered recent coronaries or have already been told that they are to be made redundant.

The typical Dance is a mixture of genuine high spirits and false bonhomie. For executives it is particularly important that they should seem, and be seen, to be having a good time so that nothing should spoil the festive atmosphere. Thus, hard headed accountants, notorious for their meanness, smile indulgently at whisky-guzzling salesmen; works managers trade jokes with marketing men; and even personnel directors unbend sufficiently to dance with the wives of management trainees.

But despite all the backslapping and frenzied togetherness, an executive should remember that he is still very much on duty. If he cannot hold his drink or, worse still, his tongue, he can cause irreparable damage to his promotion prospects. For this is no time to buttonhole his boss about a salary increase or tell a risqué story to the MD's wife, nor should he dance too closely with nubile secretaries. But perhaps the biggest temptation of all in such a convivial atmosphere is to 'sound off' at the bar about company policies. Such a man cannot complain if retribution comes quickly. Everyone knows that booze is the mother of truth.

By all means have a good time but remain on your guard: do nothing which could be construed as immature behaviour. Drink sparingly, circulate freely, and remain calm even when some besotted office junior spills rum and coca-cola over your hired evening dress. Suits can be laundered but not reputations. And it is, after all, the season of goodwill.

The company outing
Many companies encourage their employees to form social clubs which provide a wide variety of recreational activities, ranging from outings to theatres, concerts, and race meetings to occasional weekends on the Costa Brava. These outings usually receive generous coverage in the company newspaper, with accompanying photographs of glassy eyed club members in various stages of alcoholic euphoria.

The interesting thing about these events is that they are rarely attended by senior management who regard them as 'bread and circuses' for the lower orders. This is hardly surprising since the atmosphere on these outings is overwhelmingly democratic: for once, Jack is as good as his master—and he is not slow to let him know it. There can be few more harrowing experiences for a status-conscious senior executive than to find himself on a coach at two in the morning, surrounded by bawling revellers and clinking bottles—particularly if he sits at the rear of the coach, the traditional setting for amorous fumbling.

Nevertheless, these outings remain extremely popular with employees since they provide a rare opportunity to break out of the straitjacket of formal company relationships. They are also the source of much highly coloured gossip which helps to stave off the boredom of daily routine and brings a touch of the exotic into humdrum lives. From the company's point of view they make a useful contribution to corporate 'togetherness'; more important still, they provide an outlet for energies which might otherwise be channelled into more subversive activities. It is no accident that some of the most flourishing social clubs exist in non-unionized companies which regard them as a valuable safeguard against industrial militancy. Thus, as often happens in business, simple events mask complex motivations. Things are rarely as straightforward as they seem.

The farewell drink

With its uniquely bitter-sweet flavour, this is one of the most fascinating of all company rituals. Officially, of course, it is a gathering of colleagues who have met to celebrate the departure of one of their number and to wish him well in his new assignment. But underneath the joking and expressions of goodwill, it is not difficult to detect the signs of future discord, based partly upon envy of the leaver's good fortune and partly upon resentment at having been left behind.

This underlying note of sourness becomes especially notable when the firm is one of those ultra-paternalistic companies which believes that employees ought to be eternally grateful for being on the payroll, as if this were some kind of exalted privilege which no man in his right senses would seek to renounce. Clearly, since they believe themselves to be offering a form of earthly paradise to their employees, such companies are often hurt and bewildered when an executive quits, particularly if he is moving to a hated competitor. This explains the frequent absences from these parties of long serving executives for whom such revelries are an act of treason.

Be that as it may, by the third round of drinks there is usually plenty of seditious talk around, centring upon the inadequacy of salaries, the meanness of the company benefits, and, above all, the incurable gormlessness of senior management. The departing executive becomes unwittingly a focal point for discontent and is assured by everyone that he is doing the right thing. 'Can't be worse than this place' is a frequent comment.

If companies could ban these gatherings they probably would since they often trigger off a spate of job hunting by men who have been thinking about taking the plunge themselves. But since this would run counter to the British tradition of good sportsmanship, they allow them to continue and hope for the best.

The beauty contest

The company beauty contest, trivial though it may appear, has a unique importance. It is one of the few concessions which management ever willingly makes to the democratic process of election to office. The fact that the winner has no executive powers is beside the point. The will of the people has, for once, prevailed.

Formerly very common during the fifties and sixties, beauty contests have declined in popularity with the advance of Women's Lib. No longer a vehicle for ambitious young typists, keen to advance to senior secretarial status, they have become a laughing stock in such companies as continue to run them. It is not only that the more liberated females refuse to take part: the younger, more independent minded executives also dislike them. The result is that they remain popular only with female exhibitionists and male voyeurs and are found mainly in companies where few women are promoted.

Nevertheless, even though they are no longer taken very seriously, it is by no means uncommon for them to cause occasional ripples of discontent, especially in companies with autocratic managements. If the winner is chosen by popular vote there is rarely a problem but if, as sometimes happens, she is selected by the chairman or managing director, then there is virtually certain to be some suspicion that the result was fixed. Such feelings are often particularly strong in companies which operate in several locations where it is felt, rightly or wrongly, that head office females have an unfair advantage. Small wonder that many companies have abandoned these contests as being divisive instead of helping to foster good employee relations. It is very doubtful whether beauty contests can survive in the present climate of female emancipation. Basically, they are a tawdry reminder of a bygone age in which a woman's efficiency mattered less than her looks.

The management conference

The company management conference is the internal equivalent of the annual general meeting of shareholders. Its purpose is to review the company's performance during the past year; to assess its prospects for the coming year; and to motivate those attending to achieve their objectives. In more staid organizations it is a highly formalistic gathering which is dominated by top management and acres of statistics. In others, especially if they are American owned, the atmosphere is as emotional as a Salvationist meeting.

The real work at such conferences takes place outside the formal sessions, notably in bars and on golf courses. Here information is exchanged, plots are hatched, alliances are cemented, and confidences are leaked. Characteristically, there is much talk of whose star is rising and whose is falling, of organizational changes and management re-shuffles, of boardroom rows and impending resignations. All these items are discussed with far more enthusiasm than any which appear on the formal agenda—not surprisingly, since they enable managers to anticipate the future and to gauge their chances of personal survival.

While it is considered an honour for a manager to be invited to address the conference, woe betide him should his presentation fail to impress: his promotion prospects will almost certainly be affected. No wonder that so many managers accept these invitations with extremely mixed feelings and worry themselves into a high state of nervousness. Conversely, a man who makes an excellent speech is often quietly marked out for future advancement, even though his managerial track record may be no more than average. Such are the quirks and injustices of business life. So often it is not just a question of 'who you know' but by whom you are heard or seen.

The retirement presentation

A retirement presentation has much in common with a funeral service: the difference is that the corpse is alive and apparently well. The atmosphere is a curious mixture of sadness and gaiety such as one often finds at pre-wedding stag parties. There is also sometimes a dash of envy contributed by those who wish that they were leaving too.

There is a well established etiquette for these occasions. The executive who is making the presentation assumes the role of TV quiz-master while the recipient plays the part of the winning contestant. The surrounding onlookers are the studio audience, ever ready to applaud the feeblest quip and thoroughly relishing their colleague's embarrassment. And who could fail to be embarrassed by the typical presentation speech with its exaggerated praise and maudlin sentiment—the kind of thing one finds on Victorian headstones? It is not easy to know the

115

truth (and to know that others know the truth) and yet to be powerless to put the record straight.

Still, this is no time for recriminations and baring the soul: it is a time for fantasy and make-believe. The fantasy, for example, that giving up work is as easy as buying a new shirt instead of the traumatic experience that it so often is. The make-believe that the departing colleague will live happily ever after in some idyllic cottage, insulated by his memories against raging inflation and finding fulfilment in pottering around the garden. Incredibly enough, since time is their great enemy, retiring staff are often given watches or clocks. Is there no end to man's inhumanity to man?

And when it is all over, this most tasteless of ceremonies, what is there left except for the fast fading memories of a departed friend or an unloved enemy? Companies should bury their dead quietly and with dignity; more important still, they should make much better provision for the realities of retirement. A first rate pension, reviewed at least annually, is worth a whole warehouse of cuckoo clocks.

There are a number of other more personalized rituals which involve individuals rather than groups. For example, there is the performance appraisal interview during which a man's performance is judged by his boss; the salary review meeting at which these judgements are converted into cash; and the 'career development' discussion which purports to enlighten him about his future prospects.

Thus, whether he likes it or not, no man is an island if he works in business: he is inevitably a member of a number of groups. If he is wise and wishes to prosper, he will participate in those rituals which he is expected to support, regardless of whether he finds them wholly congenial. After all, there is a kind of strength in being a member of a crowd. The lonely individualist is much more vulnerable.

116

15.

The company exorcists

What are these,
So withered and so wild in their attire,
That look not like th' inhabitants o' the earth,
And yet are on't?

Shakespeare, *Macbeth*, Act I, Scene I

The recent revival of public interest in things occult and supernatural must strike many experienced managers as absurdly overheated, if not downright boring. After all, companies have long employed various types of white collar exorcists to cast out demons and ward off evil spirits: indeed, whole new departments have been created for precisely this purpose. Some of these groups operate in specialized technical areas, others are more concerned with human problems. Essentially, their task is to root out and destroy those malignant forces which are thought to be threatening the wellbeing of the company. And there is rarely a lack of devils.

The company psychologist
In large organizations the company psychologist acts as a kind of one man barrier against external infections. Often employed to interview candidates for executive jobs, his task is to detect those applicants who would be unlikely to adapt to the corporate culture. Sometimes he can easily identify potential 'subversives' through some tell tale aspect of their dress or speech, but there are many others who cannot be so easily unmasked.

It is then that he must fall back upon the tools of his trade, in particular, the dreaded psychological questionnaire. The effect of these tests is to lull the candidate into a false sense of security by presenting him with a liberal choice of answers to every question, all of which appear to be equally desirable. Unfortunately for the candidate, this is far from the case, since his answers are then matched against a large number of 'personality profiles', often ranging from directors to hard core criminals.

Such tests are generally very successful in maintaining the uniformity of the company's managerial cadre. For example, woe betide any applicant for a sales management job who scores high on intellectual and artistic interests as opposed to the more robust delights of outdoor sports (it is, after all, a well known fact that the devil finds work for overactive brains). Similarly, those who show a liking for more solitary pursuits are thought unlikely to join enthusiastically in such important company rituals as the Christmas Dance.

The success of the psychologist in exorcizing such external demons largely explains the reluctance of those managers who are already on the payroll to submit themselves to these tests, especially when it is suspected that they are being used for internal promotion purposes. And the more senior the manager the greater the resistance; understandably, since such men have far more to lose if the results are unfavourable. Indeed, is it doubtful whether some of our most successful entrepreneurs would have survived such tests taken at an earlier stage in their careers.

The public relations officer

All companies have a horror of bad publicity, and not without reason. Quite apart from the effect upon the share price, a company with a poor corporate image is likely to have great difficulty in recruiting staff of the requisite calibre. Thus, the more notorious 'hire and fire' organizations are forced to pay premium salaries (which, in effect, contain a strong element of 'danger money') in order to obtain their share of the available executive talent.

The role of the PRO is to preserve the purity of his company's image or, if it has already been besmirched, to make the best of a bad job. Either way, this means that he must remain constantly alert to exorcize those impish demons who can all too easily wreck a press release or cause an official company statement to be greeted with gales of ribald laughter. It is a thankless task. Long hours must be spent in checking galley proofs for printer's gremlins, in searching for *non-sequiturs* in the chairman's speech and above all in avoiding that nightmare which haunts all PRO's—a hostile question in the House.

Life as a PRO can be, and often is, nasty, brutish, and short. Indeed, in some companies the decimation of the PR department has come to be regarded as an annual event. The reason for this is generally not incompetence nor, for the most part, emotional instability: the sad fact is that the PR man makes the perfect scapegoat. All too often he is not privy to the real intention of the company and is denied access to vital information. He is simply regarded as a smooth purveyor of company bromides which hard bitten journalists are expected to swallow without question. Small wonder that the PRO frequently succumbs to the very demons he seeks to exorcize.

The management trainer

The management trainer is the chief salesman of the great management dream factory. Both prophet and missionary, he tells wondrous tales of a new golden age of management in which all executives will be logical, rational, and completely devoted to the company's interests. His evangelistic fervour is equalled only by his naiveté. To enter into the kingdom of the 'effective manager', all that is needed, it would seem, is that you should manage by objectives, motivate your subordinates, and delegate large chunks of your job at every conceivable opportunity.

The principal demon which the management trainer seeks to exorcize is that fiend in human form, the autocratic manager. Here, we are told is the root of all industrial evil, the progenitor of strikes, absenteeism, low productivity, high labour turnover, and nearly all executive neuroses. Yet for all his many sins, such a man is not beyond redemption. If only he will learn to 'communicate' with his subordinates and consult them when making decisions, he will readily be accepted into the ranks of the righteous. And great will be the rejoicing at the company's management training centre.

Unhappily, executive leopards do not change their spots so easily; indeed, why should they when so many of them are so comfortably ensconced on the upper branches of the management tree? It is this awful dichotomy between management theory and corporate practice which transforms so many management trainers from enthusiastic prophets of a brave new world into frustrated, cynical nihilists, old before their time. After all, it is difficult to go on preaching that managerial crime does not pay when a cursory glance upwards shows that it can indeed.

Nevertheless, for the really dedicated management trainer, there is always a better tomorrow. He has the consolation of knowing that, if he can succeed in casting out the devils from today's management trainees, the result may be a more enlightened senior management in ten years' time.

The accountant

The accountant spends his life locked in mortal combat with the twin demons of waste and extravagance. By temperament he is one of nature's Roundheads, a spartan, puritanical figure who is deeply resentful of the Cavalier excesses of his colleagues in sales and marketing. Indeed, there are few tasks which he enjoys more than vetting salesmen's expense accounts.

The trouble with the accountant is that in his praiseworthy crusade against waste he frequently produces remedies which are worse than the disease. He is a past master of creating elaborate 'control systems' which save pennies but cost pounds. He is the arch-apostle of putting everything in writing, so that in organizations where his influence is strong the entrepreneurial spirit is a weak, sickly creature, hemmed in by countless *verbotens* in the form of written policies and instructions. The result is that managerial risk taking becomes a thing of the past as managers concentrate upon solving internal problems instead of grasping external opportunities.

But in his never ending war against the demon of waste the accountant has one great advantage over his fellow exorcists: he can generally quantify his arguments. Not for him the extravagant optimism of the PRO or the childlike faith of the management trainer. 'Not only am I right', he says, 'but here are the figures to prove it.' It is because of his adroit and often ruthless use of his numerate skills that the accountant so frequently triumphs over those who can only offer feelings, opinions, and moral sentiments. And such is the veneration of most non-accounting managers for what the figures 'prove' that, even when events show that he was wrong, his credibility rarely suffers any long term damage. The power of his mystique is far too strong.

Unquestionably the accountant is a most influential company exorcist and one of the very few who cuts much ice with busy line managers. Armed with an impressive battery of accounting rituals, he is supremely well equipped to fight fire with fire; so much so that he is regarded, perhaps unfairly, by many as an even greater demon than those he seeks to vanquish.

The personnel officer

The personnel officer performs a dual function as an exorcist. First, like the company psychologist, he is concerned to prevent undesirable elements from penetrating the organization (though he generally operates at a far lower level of recruitment). Secondly, in his industrial relations role, he attempts to limit the amount of mischief caused by those demons who have somehow eluded the company's selection checkpoints. Thus, much of his time is spent in monitoring the activities of shop floor 'subversives' and taking appropriate counter-measures to frustrate their ploys.

As an exorcist, there are two basic options open to him. He can either elect to wait for such demons to expose themselves and then take action; or he can try to out-think and outmanoeuvre them by anticipating the kind of issues which are likely to cause trouble. The latter strategy is usually by far the more successful, since experience shows that those who prefer to play a waiting game are likely to be confronted by situations which are virtually out of control. Indeed, it is the Micawber-like tendencies of some personnel officers (condoned, if not encouraged, by higher management) which have turned many a tiny acorn of an issue into a towering oak tree of dissent—one which threatens to crush the entire organization.

Like his half-brother, the management trainer, the personnel officer often finds that many of his problems have been caused by the incompetence and intransigence of line management. All too often, by the time that he arrives upon the scene clutching numerous copies of the union agreement, great fires of discontent are burning fiercely in practically every part of the factory. And since he is normally equipped to deal only with small fires, and even smaller demons, it is hardly surprising that such disputes invariably have to be settled on a higher level. The personnel officer, then, is rarely more than a minor exorcist, a fact which is only too well understood by the more militant of his opponents.

The chairman
In contrast to the other exorcists, who operate at humbler levels in the organization, the chairman deals only with those top level demons who threaten the very survival of the company itself. His main forte lies in resisting the onslaughts of those particularly cunning imps who delight in undermining the 'confidence' of the City and the investing public. He is the arch-defender of the corporate holy grail.

Every year he presides over that most impressive of all exorcist ceremonies, the annual general meeting. Here he offers up thanks to those benevolent angels who have watched over the company's destiny

('I am happy to report that we have had another good year'), while at the same time acknowledging the perennial challenge of the powers of darkness ('recent government regulations are likely to be reflected in lower profit margins during the coming quarter'). If he is in a particularly aggressive mood, he may even take the opportunity of launching a vitriolic counter-attack upon that prince of demons, 'inflation', and his notorious henchmen 'escalating wage costs' and 'industrial militancy'. Invariably, he will conclude the ceremony by pronouncing his blessing upon both directors and staff in recognition of their outstanding loyalty and steadfastness during the previous twelve months.

As befits his role as the company's chief exorcist, the chairman surrounds himself with assorted paraphernalia designed to ward off the evil eye. Portraits of past company chairmen gaze down at him from the walls of his office. Lining the shelves of the bookcase are some of the great sacred texts of such revered prophets as Drucker and Herzberg. Not least, resplendent in its corner, is the well stocked cocktail cabinet, the source of much spiritual comfort in the fight against evil. All these items are not, as some cynics have suggested, mere empty status symbols: they are the necessary tools of a chief exorcist's trade.

Emperor of all he surveys, defender of the corporate faith, the chairman carries a heavy burden of responsibility which is made no lighter by those who carp about the size of his salary or the munificence of his benefits. A man more to be pitied than envied, he is the company's chief bulwark against the sinister forces in the external environment.

The question remains: 'Is it possible for a company to continue to be "possessed" in spite of the efforts of its internal exorcists?' Indeed it is; and for proof one need only recall some of the more traumatic mergers and takeovers of the past decade. No doubt in many of these cases the devil merely claimed what was due to him, his task made easier by boardroom wrangling and management incompetence. But, happily, there are many other instances of disaster being averted because of the timely intervention of powerful external exorcists, namely *consultants*.

The well publicized successes of some consultancy firms in sniffing out and vanquishing some pretty obdurate corporate demons has made their services *de rigueur* for many large organizations, not least in the public sector. Whether their efforts will have any lasting effect only time will tell (presumably not even the proudest would claim to drive away *all* managerial devils). But at least they can help to bring down the victim's temperature and do some much needed physiotherapy while he regains his spiritual and physical strength. Sometimes that is enough.

16.

'Unaccustomed as I am'

For I have neither wit, nor words, nor worth,
Action, nor utterance, nor power of speech,
To stir men's blood; I only speak right on;
I tell you that which you yourselves do know.

Shakespeare, *Julius Caesar*, Act III, Scene II

Every year hundreds of organizations hold their annual conferences which are regarded as the highlight of the company's year. Vast sums are lavished upon five star hotels and no effort is spared to produce a lively agenda. Frequently, a number of guest speakers are invited to these meetings to inject new thinking into the corporate bloodstream. Regardless of differences in their individual backgrounds, most can be grouped into six main types.

The distinguished amateur

This man may be knowledgeable about many subjects but not, alas, the one which appears on the agenda. His presence is frequently the result of a business lunch when in a moment of madness he agreed to speak. Bitterly regretting this act of folly, he has lain awake at nights worrying about his speech ever since.

Often a senior executive with a major company, it is hoped that he will reveal his organization's recipe for success. Unhappily, as he bumbles from cliché to cliché, it would appear that greatness has been thrust upon him and that he is exceedingly fortunate to be where he is. Curiously enough, his very ineptitude tends to encourage those members of the audience who aspire to the board. After all, they reason, if such a man can climb so high even the moderately talented need not give up hope.

This type of speaker does least damage if he is brought on immediately after lunch since most of the audience will be half asleep. Alternatively, he can be used as an after-dinner speaker when audiences are traditionally more tolerant of feeble jokes.

The expert

Never engage a man simply because of his reputation in his field. The fact that he has written a definitive book or published an influential article is no guarantee of his platform ability. Indeed, the greater his erudition the more likely it is that he will fail to communicate since he will invariably overestimate his audience's knowledge.

It does not take long for such a man to make his mark. Within a few minutes of his ponderous introduction, eyes grow weary and heads begin to nod. Outbreaks of coughing spread like the plague. The chairman, poor wretch, trapped by his office, starts taking notes in an effort to keep awake. When refreshments arrive the audience reacts like a beleaguered garrison which has just caught sight of the relieving column. Taking advantage of the scramble for tea, some of the bolder spirits melt away and are last seen heading for the hotel lounge.

With few exceptions, experts tend to live in a world of their own, engrossed in the minutiae of their specialization. It is no use bewailing their shortcomings as communicators. Most of them are unaware that any problems exist.

The showman

This man is a particular favourite at sales conferences where his earthy sense of humour is greatly appreciated. Often a former salesman himself, he can revitalize even the dullest meeting with his hilarious anecdotes and merry quips.

He is nothing if not versatile. The actor's gestures, the comedian's sense of timing, the con man's plausibility—these are the tools of his trade and he uses them with the skill of a master craftsman. He is totally impervious to sarcasm and irony and can quell any interruption with a deadly *ad lib*. And yet such is his aura of bubbling good fellowship that he never once loses his audience's goodwill. On the contrary, he is readily accepted as 'one of the boys', a man with whom they can identify completely.

Never ask him to speak on a serious subject; he is needlessly handicapped if required to be profound. Accept him simply for what he is, a genial entertainer with no delusions of grandeur whose purpose is to provide some light relief.

The package merchant
There is no mistaking this man: he is one of the most prolific speakers on the conference circuit. But like a concert pianist with a limited repertoire he gives virtually the same performance on every occasion.

However, within his narrow range, he is the complete professional and delivers his message with impeccable flair. Each vocal intonation is carefully rehearsed, each dramatic gesture faultlessly timed. While he holds the floor he is well-nigh invincible but at question time he is much more vulnerable since his limited experience is more easily exposed. It is then that he often becomes tetchy and aggressive, seeking to bludgeon his critics into a respectful silence.

He is generally more popular with younger managers who are captivated by his professional skill. More experienced executives, interested in deeds not words, are likely to find him a garrulous bore.

The academic
Academics frequently have great difficulty in establishing rapport with business groups. Accustomed to addressing captive audiences, they rarely attempt to sell their ideas and seem particularly allergic to simple language.

Many give displays of intellectual gymnastics which leave their audiences thoroughly confused. Every opinion is cocooned with so many qualifications that it is difficult to know what they really believe. Annoying, too, is their habit of quoting learned authorities whose names are meaningless to most executives and who often seem more expert at motivating rodents than in dealing with the problems of businessmen.

Most disastrous of all is the would-be humorist who peppers his audience with donnish puns. The fact that these fall flat never seems to worry him and he plods on regardless of his icy reception. No doubt he feels that it is not his fault if too few executives have been properly educated.

The professional
You can always recognize a real professional: when approached he invariably states his fee before agreeing to speak. He will also point out that this figure is exclusive of expenses, nor does it cover the supply of any course notes.

Expensive though he is, he gives excellent value for money and quickly impresses even the most cynical group. Tough, aggressive, and brimming with self-confidence, he revels in the challenge of hostile questioning and defends himself verbally with both stiletto and club. For many audiences, the highlight of his performance is when he cuts down to size some much feared senior manager who is labouring under the delusion that he is an effective executive. Certainly, he is no respecter of persons; not even managing directors are immune from his lash.

Another mark of the professional is that he usually sends in his bill within a week of his talk. It is wise to pay him promptly for if there is any delay he will not hesitate to contact the chairman himself.

One final point. Remember, there is no sense in hiring a potential conference wrecker simply because he is temptingly cheap. After all, you would not expect to find a masterpiece in a bargain basement. Like most things in business you tend to get what you pay for. And if you pick the wrong speaker then you really pay for what you get.

17.

The expendables

Cheer up, the worst is yet to come.

Philander Chase Johnson, *Shooting Stars*

When business is booming everyone is happy and there seems never a cloud on the horizon. It is at times like these that companies grow fat and complacent, intoxicated by the euphoria of apparently endless success. But sooner or later comes the day of reckoning: a recession sets in. The effect is immediate. Smiles vanish, brows become furrowed, and words like 'retrenchment' and 'redundancy' are on everyone's lips. Executives who formerly swung a carefree golf club on Wednesday afternoons or took the occasional day off at the local race course now huddle together and exchange grapevine gossip.

All, of course, are potentially vulnerable but some are much more vulnerable than others. At greatest risk are those executives whose results can be measured and those who provide a service which is no longer needed. They are the ones who come under the most critical scrutiny. The heroes of yesterday become the scapegoats of today.

The sales manager

The sales manager is widely regarded by his more envious colleagues as an unbridled hedonist who lives off the company. With his company car and expense account lunches, his trips abroad and his luxury hotels, he seems like a member of the industrial jet-set to those who rarely escape from their desks. All this, however, is mere surface gloss. He is one of the most vulnerable members of the management team.

It is not difficult to see why this should be so. Those who live by the sword often die by the sword and the sales manager is a master of verbal swordplay. He it is who offers up that annual sacrifice to the gods of chance, the sales forecast, and who mesmerizes his masters with his perennial optimism. If he achieves his targets, all well and good; if not, then he becomes the perfect scapegoat. This is the reason why his 'perks' are justified; not because he is more gifted than anyone else. When disaster is a mere knife's throw away, he can hardly be blamed for living well.

While some sales managers are downright incompetent and have only themselves to thank for their constant misfortunes, many others are much more sinned against than sinning. A general market downturn, an ill-judged price increase, a revolutionary new product introduced by a competitor—such factors can cause even the best men to fail. Nevertheless, the sales manager can hardly complain if his excuses are brushed aside: he is notoriously intolerant of mistakes by others. Let an order be lost or a delivery date missed and he will descend upon the offender like an ill tempered bear, roundly berating him for his carelessness and incompetence. No wonder that there are smiles when he falls from grace. He who beats the drum must sometimes carry the can.

The recruiter

Here is another highly vulnerable executive, particularly if he deals with management recruitment. It takes only a few poor performances by executives whom he has selected to cause critical eyes to be turned in his direction. After all, an adviser is judged by the quality of his advice and if he advises badly then he must expect retribution.

Like the sales manager, the recruiter is often the victim of his own shortcomings. All too often he tends to play it safe and to reject those applicants who might be 'difficult to manage'. The result is that the organization quickly fills up with men who are totally non-creative and have about as much entrepreneurial drive as a minor civil servant. While business remains buoyant, such errors rarely show but once a recession sets in they become extremely visible. And who better to blame for an executive's incompetence than the man who was responsible for bringing him into the company?

Naturally, it is not always incompetence that causes a recruiter to be dismissed. For example, if a company places an embargo upon recruitment as part of a general cost cutting exercise, then the reason for his job ceases to exist. And if he cannot easily be redeployed elsewhere, and few recruiters have many other marketable skills, then he will soon be reading the appointments columns. The moral for recruiters, as for any other specialist, is that they should make every effort to broaden their experience and not stay too long in such a restricted role. It may be satisfying to act as both judge and jury but when the laws are suspended who needs either?

The advertising man

Even during normal times the advertising manager occupies one of the most precarious rungs on the executive ladder; in a recession his position can become positively lethal. The trouble is that virtually every director has his own ideas on how best to project the company's image or to present the product to its various publics. Consequently, there is never a lack of 'I-told-you-so's' whenever things go wrong. It is like trying to conduct an orchestra composed entirely of conductors.

In some large corporations the advertising man may be empowered to direct his own campaigns; but in most companies he is simply the middleman between the Board and the agency. This means that he is constantly at the mercy of so-called 'creative professionals' whose managerial abilities may leave much to be desired. For example, it is by no means unknown for a new product to be launched at a 'press conference' at which no journalists are present, the agency having forgotten to send out the invitations. Another typical debacle is when vital advertisements fail to be published on the scheduled dates, due to poor communications between the agency and the newspapers. Yet no matter who has blundered, one thing is certain: the advertising manager will be held responsible.

All this would not matter so much if only he were able to measure his results, but advertising is a notoriously imprecise area, not given to the certainties of sales statistics. In addition, there are still many executives who regard such expenditures as money down the drain, mere fripperies which contribute nothing to profits. The result is that in times of crisis he is like a soldier caught in the open by enemy machine guns, with some of his own comrades directing their fire.

The training officer

Although not quite as vulnerable as he used to be, the training officer still occupies one of the hottest seats in business. Like his colleague, the advertising executive, he shares a common disability in rarely being able to quantify his results. Similarly, he will quickly encounter numerous executives who consider that training is a waste of time. But there is one additional burden which the training man carries that no other 'expendable' is required to shoulder. He can only do his job when others stop doing theirs.

The problem of ensuring that enough people are released to attend his courses is probably the biggest single headache of the training officer's job. All too often an executive who has promised to release a number of his subordinates will withdraw them from the course at the eleventh hour, leaving the trainer with the unenviable choice of either cancelling the course or running it for a handful of the original trainees. And when he protests about such imperious actions he will be told unequivocally that 'the job comes first', which is simply an excuse for a failure to plan. Indeed, for the trainer it is a classic 'Catch 22' situation. If he fails to run courses he is accused of being idle but when he attempts to run them he is denied support.

Nevertheless, some training men create their own misfortunes by promising a good deal more than they are able to deliver. This is especially true of those endemic panacea-mongers, the management trainers, who frequently rampage through their companies like hellfire preachers, promising miraculous transformations within a matter of days. When these brave new worlds fail to materialize, they invariably become the butt of much ferocious criticism, for hell hath no fury like an executive conned. It is hardly surprising that during a business downturn their services should be regarded as highly dispensable. Men who seem to thrive upon self-inflicted wounds ought not to complain when others wield the knife.

The marketing manager

Ask a dozen marketing experts for their definitions of marketing and the chances are that you will receive twelve very different replies. For some, it means being consumer rather than product oriented; others simply see it as a branch of sales. But regardless of the merits of any particular philosophy, one thing is certain: if the theoreticians are divided then the practitioners are *confused*.

During the past decade the marketing function (whatever it may be) has attracted the attentions of motivational researchers, way-out sociologists, erudite mathematicians, and ambitious business graduates. In large corporations it has assumed the proportions of a monastic order, dedicated to esoteric rituals which purport to be scientific. In fact, for all its regression analyses, Markov chains, and input–output tables,

136

marketing remains essentially a judgemental process in which an ounce of flair is worth a ton of theory. Its major contribution has been to pose one vital question: 'What business are we in?' And it has sometimes succeeded in answering even that question badly.

Of late, many marketing men have suffered the fate which awaits every witch doctor when his magic begins to wane: they have lost face, and some have even been expelled from their tribes. This growing disenchantment with marketing specialists is at present only partially reflected in the job vacancy columns (since to be disillusioned with a particular witch doctor does not necessarily imply a disbelief in magic). But increasingly, in the here and now of competitive warfare, the life of a marketeer can be and often is nasty, brutish, and short. The survivors are those who arouse the fewest expectations.

The corporate planner

The corporate planner is still a fairly rare species, being found mainly in vast international organizations with major links with the business schools. To a large extent he is a management hybrid: part accountant, part economist, part business man, part bureaucrat. Like the marketing man, he is one of the company's official clairvoyants but works on an infinitely broader canvas. His job is to anticipate fluctuations in the business cycle and make appropriate recommendations to the top decision makers.

It is a thankless task. There are, after all, so many imponderable economic variables which can quickly make nonsense of even the best laid plans. As if this were not enough, he is frequently plagued by uncooperative colleagues, many of whom regard him as an expensive trendy whose mission in life is to generate paperwork. This can lead to a kind of stealthy sabotage which can effectively prevent him from doing his job: inaccurate statistics, delayed reports, and requests for information virtually ignored. Once again, however, it is the unrealistic expectations of senior management which is so often the root cause of the planner's downfall. The idea that one man, however high powered, can successfully predict the behaviour of gigantic market forces is patently absurd. Indeed, it would be laughable were not the consequences of failure frequently so drastic for the individuals concerned. Many a corporate planner must have sighed with Lear, 'As flies to wanton boys are we to the gods; they kill us for their sport'.

The other main culprits, of course, are those erudite management theorists for whom business is a chessboard and the managers mere pawns. In the hothouse world of the MBA Seminar all things seem

137

possible; no fortress looks impregnable, no problem insoluble. All too often the corporate planner is hoist not by his own but by someone else's petard; the professor who convinced the chairman that the job was viable.

The research scientist

There are two broad categories of scientist in industry: those who do pure research aimed at creating new products and those who work mainly on product development. During a recession both groups are likely to have their numbers thinned out, particularly those who are working on long term projects with little immediate prospect of a return upon investment.

Research scientists are among the most professional and dedicated of all white collar workers but they labour under two principal disadvantages, both of which can prove lethal when times are hard. First, they are often incredibly badly managed and poorly motivated, frequently working on the sketchiest of briefs with no clear-cut objectives or target dates. Secondly, being engrossed in their work, they fail to keep their political fences in good repair so that their voice is rarely heard at the highest echelons. This means that axe wielding accountants can scythe through their budgets with very little risk of meeting a determined challenge. And since much research work is inevitably futuristic, it is often difficult to point to any immediate consequences which are likely to prove disastrous to the firm's profitability.

The result is that the lambs of research are duly slaughtered while less valuable specimens escape the axe. The remedy, of course, lies in the research man's own hands. Instead of isolating himself from the mainstream of the company and affecting a puritanical disdain for political infighting, he should exert the same pressures as any other executive to ensure that his interests are not overlooked. For example, he should demand that he receives proper management training, not fight like fury to avoid attending such courses. Equally important, he should insist upon being managed more effectively by his own superiors, and he can hardly do this unless he knows what good management is. In short, he should leave his ivory tower and come in from the cold. Men do not survive in business by knowledge alone.

Not every executive is gravely threatened by a recession: indeed some bloom like orchids during a tropical storm. Accountants, for example, are in their element, sniffing out 'waste' like over-zealous bloodhounds and recommending economies which affect everyone but themselves. Then there are those so-called 'efficiency experts' who, armed with stopwatch and slide rule, lurk in gangways and quiet corners of offices, ever ready to pounce upon human imperfection. But do not begrudge them their brief moments of glory. They also serve who only stand and prate.

18.

The meetings men

But far more numerous was the herd of such
Who think too little and who talk too much.

John Dryden, Absalom and Achitophel

For many executives meetings are a waste of time, a boring diversion from the job of managing. And yet, while it is true that meetings are often unproductive, they can provide many valuable insights into executive behaviour. Here, as in few other situations, can your political skills be used to the full and lessons be learned from more practised colleagues. Equally, you can learn from others' defeats and resolve not to make the same kinds of mistake. And gradually, as you serve your apprenticeship, you begin to recognize the following types.

The Manipulator
Particularly prominent in boardroom meetings, the Manipulator is a master of political swordplay. He always knows exactly what he wants and thoroughly researches any proposal he makes. He applies a simple test to any idea: 'Does it advance or threaten my personal interests?' The answer determines which way he argues; the company's interest is a secondary matter.

The Manipulator's power rests upon three great strengths. First, he is a highly skilled communicator who uses words with precision and flair. Secondly, he has a gift for personal diplomacy, never seeking to crush his opponents in debate but to make it easy for them to change their minds. Thirdly, he is a shrewd psychologist who knows the weaknesses of everyone present and can effectively turn them to his own advantage, like a smooth politician dealing with questions.

Never too forthright, nor too self-effacing, he makes a point of never losing his temper, no matter how much he may be fuming inwardly. He suffers fools not merely gladly but even joyfully since he can invariably convert them into supporting him. He knows that even the stoutest defences can be undermined by judicious flattery. He is never too tired to massage an ego or to soothe the prickings of a guilty conscience.

The Manipulator is born to succeed; with his kind of talent he can hardly fail. While others argue he bides his time until the moment is ripe for him to intervene. Then, when confusion is at its height and his opponents are divided, he strikes with all the deadliness of an angry cobra, though he is careful not to let his emotions show through. His proposal is accepted by his exhausted colleagues and his reputation as a statesman takes another step forward. It is not so much that he divides and conquers as he allows others to divide and conquer themselves.

The Refugee

The Refugee is an inveterate attender of meetings; they are a welcome balm to his self-importance. He uses them to escape from his day-to-day problems, particularly the need to make decisions. Meetings become for him a second home, a cosy refuge from the storms outside. He is not concerned with what is on the agenda; he is happy enough to have been invited.

As an *aficionado* of meetings, he knows most of the tricks and is especially adept at prolonging discussions. Regardless of whether he knows anything about it, he will offer his opinions on almost any subject, even though they never have the slightest effect. Indeed, once he starts speaking, his colleagues switch off and seem to regard his intervention as the signal for a break. There are more glazed eyes during his ponderous platitudes than in a classroom of children doing a mathematics test.

Be that as it may, there is method in his madness; the meeting is prevented from breaking up early. Since this is always his primary objective, he is a fervent advocate of 'working parties' which will, of course, generate further meetings. He will often volunteer to take part in such studies and to carry out any necessary research. This is not because he is academically inclined; it just allows him to spend more time off the job.

Back in his department everything is in chaos since there are some decisions which he alone can take. But gradually his subordinates learn to cope and unofficial leaders begin to emerge. This in turn makes him extremely vulnerable when the Board is thinking of swinging the axe. It may be difficult to sack a competent executive but not one who is rarely, if ever, missed.

The Guru

Here is a man who is narrow, parochial, and overspecialized. For him the world revolves around his specialist subject and he is virtually illiterate on any other topic. He is incapable of communicating in non-technical language and has difficulty in grasping abstract concepts. Wholly bereft of subtlety himself, the machinations of others are lost upon him. He is obsessed by what he calls 'scientific facts' and is not interested in things which cannot be measured.

At the slightest excuse he will submerge his colleagues beneath a tidal wave of gobbledygook which he usually delivers at machine gun speed. Oblivious of yawns and unfriendly looks, he rambles on as though he were giving a lecture and has the pedant's dislike of being interrupted. He can become very emotional if his ideas are rejected since to him they are just plain common sense. Being totally insensitive to political factors, he sees every issue in black-and-white terms.

The Guru is at heart a simpleton who is out of his depth in general business matters. Nevertheless, as a technical expert he is well respected and can be relied on to give an honest opinion. He is always worth having on your side provided that you can keep his enthusiasm in check. Make sure that he keeps to his specialized brief, otherwise he is certain to ruin your case.

The Missionary

Many executives dislike heated arguments; the Missionary positively revels in combat. Always bursting with new ideas, he conducts a one man campaign against the forces of inertia and has a knack of dramatizing even the most trivial issues. Unfortunately, he tends not to think through his ideas and is easily caught out on questions of detail. He is like a politician with a great vision of the future who has omitted to work out what his plans will cost.

Essentially he is a lovable, well meaning windbag with plenty of ideas but no sense of proportion. He changes his mind as often as his socks and can never be relied upon to take a consistent stand. Since he always neglects to do his homework, he is easily deflated by his more hard headed colleagues but never seems to learn from these bitter experiences. With amazing resilience, he returns to the attack—only to suffer yet another defeat.

With friends like the Missionary you do not need enemies; he is a natural lightweight who is easily brushed aside. But never make the error of thrashing him in debate; there is no surer way of offending your colleagues. For although he is regarded as a little soft in the head, he is usually well liked for his endearing naiveté. A mascot to be tolerated rather than a foe to be vanquished, he has many charming personal qualities.

The Volcano

The Volcano is a man born out of his time; he would have made an ideal henchman for Genghis Khan. Totally incapable of rational discussion, he despises the niceties of civilized debate and is only really at home when giving orders. His style of advocacy is painfully simple: he repeats himself but in a louder voice.

Not surprisingly, he is an abysmal politician and has no idea how to cajole or persuade. Rugged, inflexible, and frequently rude, he bull-dozes those who disagree with him with a potent mixture of sarcastic invective and explosive outbreaks of four letter words. He is, in short, an executive barbarian who should never have been allowed to rise so high. The fact that he is in charge of people at all is an indictment of the company's promotion system.

He is a man of many hates but few constructive ideas. For him all the troubles of the company can be traced to a few basic 'errors', notably its tendency to 'mollycoddle' the staff. He will work his fixations into almost any discussion with a complete disregard for their relevance to the topic. And yet, for all his forcefulness and table-pounding eloquence, he is easy meat for the skilful Manipulator who knows that flattery is his Achilles' heel. Gratified that someone appears to recognize his worth, he is often the Manipulator's strongest ally.

The Sleeper

The Sleeper is the dormouse of the management meeting, an executive who has come in from the cold. Often a long serving employee who is nearing retirement, he is resigned to the futility of most business meetings and resolutely refuses to be drawn into arguments. An elder statesman without any statesmanship, he is only present because of his senior status, which sometimes means that he has to take the chair.

His normal defence mechanism during meetings is to doze sedately for hours on end without ever actually falling asleep. As he daydreams fitfully about his retirement cottage, he seems totally unaware of the battles around him; not even the Volcano can bring him to life. His sole contribution to any meeting is usually to announce the arrival of tea. He could not care less which side wins so long as he is left to dream in peace.

While universally liked for his gentlemanly manners, the Sleeper is an executive who is clearly 'past it'; he is just playing out time until his pension. He is not worth lobbying for his support since he has no intention of becoming involved. 'Let sleeping dogs lie' is his personal motto and he does his best to live up to it. He is interested neither in rebels nor causes and is perfectly happy with things as they are.

The Bureaucrat

This man likes tidy, well disciplined meetings with proper minutes and rules of order. A great nit-picker and master quibbler, he has an unrivalled capacity for missing the point and is one of the primary reasons why meetings drag on. Totally devoid of all vision and flair, he is an arch-opponent of anything original, his own creativity being practically nil. He can always be relied upon to slow things down and to pour cold water on others' enthusiasm.

Often possessing an administrative background, he has usually worked his way up from a clerical function. Years of dealing with invoices and order numbers have left him with a horror of taking risks and with an obsessive interest in petty costs. He feels himself surrounded by spendthrifts and wastrels who have no idea of the value of money. He sees himself as a financial St George, perpetually slaying the dragons of waste.

Being a first class natural negative thinker, he always concentrates his fire upon problems and snags. No matter how imaginative a proposal may be, he is sure to query it on the grounds of cost. He is also a great point-of-order merchant and likes to display his legal vocabulary. He is forever adding 'riders' and proposing 'motions' and complaining that someone is *ultra vires*. A glacial character without a trace of humour, he would have made an excellent solicitor's clerk.

The Compromiser

The Compromiser is the great peacemaker at meetings, a healer of wounds and soother of egos. Disliking any form of confrontation, he believes that there is always a 'happy medium' which once discovered can cure all ills. He is the least likely of men to take a stand on principle since he believes such actions to be basically futile. What matters to him is not winning battles but preventing such conflicts from taking place.

The trouble is that life in business cannot always be sweetness and light; there are times when convictions have to be fought for. The Compromiser, however, wants to run a 'happy ship' in which good human relations are all important. He therefore aims for totally spurious 'agreements' which only succeed in obscuring the issues. He would rather sweep everything under the carpet than see angry managers 'shooting it out'.

As a member of a meeting his greatest virtue is that he can sometimes help to bring the temperature down and create an atmosphere for rational discussion. As a chairman he is insipid and weak, ever ready to yield to the strongest pressure. He is easily intimidated by the Volcano's tantrums and is equally afraid of the Bureaucrat. In fact, he is far too 'nice' a guy to have any real hope of not finishing last.

While many companies suffer from meetings mania, there are a few where such gatherings are comparatively rare. Here 'management by diktat' is the prevailing style and participative methods are virtually unknown. To be invited to a meeting in such a concern is a sure-fire sign that you are on your way up. The time to worry is when your deputy is invited; you can be equally certain that you are on your way out.

19.

Out of the frying pan

At last he rose and twitch'd his mantle blue;
Tomorrow to fresh woods, and pastures new.

John Milton, *Lycidas*

From time to time almost every executive becomes disenchanted with his present job and wonders whether the grass is any greener beyond the next hill. Sometimes it may be a missed promotion that provides the spur or an impossible boss or the desire to earn more money. Whatever the reason, if you are thinking of moving, you will need to face up to a number of questions or you could well be making a disastrous mistake.

For example, what sort of organization are you interested in joining? Do you know what makes such companies tick? What kind of atmosphere do you find most congenial? Do you thrive upon pressure or dislike taking risks? For make no mistake: these are the really important issues, not simply your ability to do the job. And unless you consider them realistically your new Shangri-la could be a bed of nails.

In industry and commerce there are, broadly speaking, six types of organizations from which you can choose. Each has its strengths and its imperfections and none is intrinsically superior to the others. It all depends upon what you are seeking and what, if anything, you are prepared to sacrifice.

Murder Incorporated
This is the sort of firm to join if you enjoy living dangerously. There is

no airy-fairy stuff about social responsibilities: you are simply there to make money for the shareholders.

The atmosphere in these organizations is like Chicago during Prohibition. At the end of every month the weaker brethren are dispensed with and soon afterwards an advertisement appears in the national press detailing the exciting opportunities which await new recruits. However, in the case of senior executive appointments, the firm is more likely to call upon the service of headhunters since to advertise openly at such regular intervals would cause even the most ingenuous job seeker to smell a rat. The headhunter's strategy is invariably aimed at massaging the ego of the prospective candidate. For example, the company may be described as 'tough, no-nonsense, and down-to-earth' or as being interested only in men who can 'get results'. Often, as a kind of executive aphrodisiac, the magic word 'dynamic' is liberally used, the implication being that you are just such a man.

To succeed in such a battleground you need two main qualities. First, you must have a Kamikaze-like devotion to the company's interests; there must be no order, however distasteful, which you are not willing to obey. Secondly, you need a natural flair for political infighting and a kind of built-in radar for detecting plots. For it is not merely the Ides of March of which you must beware in such companies. *Any* day you could be accosted, Caesar-like, on your way to a meeting and your most trusted friend and colleague could turn out to be your Brutus. In short, it is a world in which you must play to win and in which nice guys, however competent, invariably come last.

Paterfamilias and Son
In complete contrast to the frenetic power play of Murder Incorporated is the feudalistic atmosphere of some family owned firms. Often located in idyllic market towns, such companies have a powerful appeal for the type of executive who is tired of the pressures of urban commuting. At first sight they would seem to offer the best of both worlds: a more gently paced job amid congenial surroundings.

Alas, would that it were always so. The frustrations may be different but they are none the less real, particularly if you have been used to working for a large organization. Many an ex-big company executive has found it difficult to adjust to the philosophies and prejudices of a family mafia. These can range from a refusal to adopt aggressive marketing policies to remuneration practices which smack of Russian roulette. One of the penalties of becoming a big fish in a much smaller pond is that you have far less water in which to swim. For example, there are all kinds of support services in large corporations which simply do not exist in many family concerns: you either do it yourself or do without. Moreover, in the more conservative companies, even your more modest proposals are likely to be resisted by men who see no need for new fangled techniques.

But in some firms perhaps the heaviest cross which you will have to bear is the assumption that you are now a member of a band of family retainers. For example, you will often find that all male members of the family expect to be addressed as 'Master' by virtually everyone below senior management level. Admittedly this practice may not affect you personally but it can create a very different ambience from the one which you have been used to. And sometimes the offshoots of this Master Race are amazingly numerous, ranging from venerable grey-beards of 80+ to apple-cheeked adolescents whose main interest in life is riding to hounds. But at least you now know where you stand. If you had doubts in your last job about your prospects of becoming chairman, here you need have no doubt at all.

National Dinosaurs

If security is your goal and you are not too irritated by bureaucracy you should consider a move to a nationalized industry. Here it is virtually impossible to buck the system and to become impatient is to risk ruining your career. Nevertheless, if you have been used to working for a high pressure firm, you may find the change agreeably restful rather like a retired rugby full-back who has taken up chess.

Remember that as an executive in a nationalized concern your primary task is to provide a service. Occasionally, while you are still new to your job, you may be tempted to close down a branch line or an uneconomic pit but these will generally prove to be only temporary aberrations. You will soon learn that there are always cogent reasons for delegating such decisions to a working party, preferably one which is unhampered by a sense of urgency. After all no true nationalizer can be a rationalizer. Your task is to preserve jobs, not to destroy them. Nevertheless, there are at least two areas in which you will need to sharpen your skills: written communications and chairmanship. You may have been taught in your previous job to express yourself in writing as succinctly as possible; if so, you must now do the opposite or you will soon be regarded as a lazy misfit. The sooner you realize that practically everything you discuss must be canonized in writing the

153

more quickly you will adjust to the prevailing culture. Similarly, you will do well to remember that most meetings are not called to get things done but to provide a welcome break from humdrum routines. It is your duty therefore to prolong them for as long as possible and to raise the kind of issues which will generate further meetings. In this way you will become known as an excellent chairman, one who refuses to be rushed into premature action.

Nitti-Gritti Engineering

Despite all those fashionable seminars about 'the marketing concept' there are still many organizations in which production is king. Dominated by engineers and watch-toting work study men, these are companies for which customers are an irritating distraction from infinitely more fascinating technical problems. 'Selling' is a word which is rarely mentioned since it is assumed that the product virtually sells itself.

There is often an 'art for art's sake' atmosphere in these organizations which makes a refreshing change from all that hard nosed concern with the results of tests and surveys which is such a feature of life in marketing-oriented companies. Here, as any engineer will tell you, life is much simpler: 'We get an idea, make a product, and hope the customer will buy it.' Naturally there is a price to be paid for such careless freedom and when times are hard the workforce is frequently decimated. This, however, is only to be expected. After all you can't hope to make trail blazing technological breakthroughs without occasionally upsetting a few careers.

In a Nitti-Gritti-type firm you must be prepared to work at constant pressure. Each day brings its quota of life shortening crises, ranging from machine breakdowns and customer complaints to overtime bans and walkouts by militant employees. Many of these traumas are entirely self-generated. For example, since there is often only the flimsiest of paperwork systems, much time is wasted in digging up facts. And when, as frequently happens, these bedlam-like conditions result in payroll errors, the scene is set for further confrontations with exasperated shop stewards who point out the weaknesses in the system for the umpteenth time. The trouble with the Nitti-Gritti firm is that management is far too busy to worry about people: they receive much less attention than the humblest machine. Not surprisingly, they react accordingly—providing yet another example of 'industrial militancy'.

Be that as it may, you would be wise to check the adequacy of your life insurance cover before you join this type of firm. A regular annual medical examination is another sensible precaution to take.

Universal Widgets Limited

Dotted around the industrial landscape, like huge, good natured pachyderms, are those mammoth combines and corporations which exert a major influence upon the national economy. Let but one of these leviathans sneeze and the City blanches: let two or three do so and we are probably heading for a major recession.

Unquestionably, many of these companies employ some of the nation's finest executive talent and have a mature awareness of their social responsibilities. The trouble is that they are so frequently the victims of their past success. Too many monopoly products and too many years of market leadership tend to take their toll and the old 'fire in the belly' begins to be replaced by a kind of organizational obesity which makes the company slow to react to its more entrepreneurial competitors. Moreover, as the colossus grows, divisions and departments proliferate like locusts, stretching lines of communication to near breaking point. It is very difficult for a manager with individualistic talents to make his mark in such a swarming antheap; nor will such individualism be particularly welcome. The requirement is for intelligent well adjusted executives who are prepared to submerge their idiosyncracies for the corporate good. A talent for boat rocking is neither prized nor rewarded.

Still, if you believe that there is safety in numbers and enjoy civilized company, a move to such a firm could be well worthwhile. It is highly unlikely that you will ever steer the ship but neither will you be left floundering in shark-infested waters. Yet another advantage of working for such companies is that you will have far more time to develop your outside interests. Whereas in Nitti-Gritti you will spend your weekends totally exhausted, here in UW Ltd you will have energy to spare with which to stomp around golf courses or mess about in boats. You are also much more likely to enjoy a lengthy retirement, fortified by a pension which is annually reviewed.

International Buccaneers

Working for a US multinational is like working for a sales-oriented Nitti-Gritti with an occasional dash of Murder Incorporated. The important thing to recognize is that you are joining a semi-religious institution which requires your conversion to its particular business theology. Nevertheless, whatever their differences in products and markets, all American companies hold at least one belief in common: there is no higher good than unlimited growth.

155

These firms are the modern equivalent of Caesar's legions, endlessly seeking new markets to conquer and tightening their grip on those they have won. To succeed you must have not merely ability but a passionate belief in the organization's mission and a willingness to work all the hours that God sends. If you wish to lead a peaceful family existence then don't become an executive in a US multinational. After all, as a soldier engaged in an economic war, you can hardly expect a ceasefire at 5 o'clock sharp.

Yet if there are sacrifices to be made there are also compensations: high salaries, excellent benefits and, not least, the kind of cameraderie that comes with membership of a winning team. Moreover, even if you should succumb to a premature coronary, rest assured that your widow's future will be financially secure: indeed she may well be given a new lease of life. In return, you must allow yourself to be shaped to the corporate mould and accept that your loyalty to the company must at all times come first.

Be careful, however, never to flaunt your educational or social background, particularly in the presence of high ranking Americans. Such men often hold deeply meritocratic beliefs and will resent any suggestion that they are being patronized. It is better to let them make the conversational running and confine yourself to topics such as motor cars and golf. For behind those bluff exteriors can lurk some pretty thin skins and it is all too easy to be labelled as a dangerous intellectual.

One final point. If none of these prospects really appeal to you, you could always, of course, become a management consultant. There is still plenty of scope for men of energy and initiative who can exude the kind of *gravitas* which inspires confidence and trust. You do not need to be overwhelmingly well qualified: indeed there are times when too much knowledge can be a positive hindrance. What you must have are tact, common sense, and a well tuned ear for the chairman's prejudices. After all he can hardly object to paying for being told that he is right.

20.

When the bough breaks

And now also the axe is laid unto the root of the trees

St Matthew ii. 10

Losing his job, whether through dismissal or redundancy, is one of the most traumatic situations that any executive can face. Not only are there financial problems to cope with: worse still is the feeling of having been thrown on the scrapheap, of no longer being a contributing citizen. And yet, human and understandable as such reactions are, there is no point in brooding over what cannot be changed. After all, provided that they are dealt with positively and creatively, today's problems can be tomorrow's opportunities.

The most important thing for an unemployed executive to recognize is that successful job hunting requires both method and flair; indeed to a large extent you create your own luck. Scanning the appointments columns is not enough: you need a variety of tactics to achieve your objective. True, there is no single approach which can guarantee success but all of the following are worth considering, so long as you avoid the more glaring pitfalls.

Dear Sir

There are three golden rules for replying to job advertisements: read the advertisement carefully, keep your reply brief, and tailor your letter to the principal job requirements. Remember that it may have to jostle for attention with many scores of competitors and must make the kind of impact that will command attention. It is in effect your first opportunity to demonstrate your calibre (and if done badly it will also be your last).

The all purpose application letter just will not do: it gives the impression that you are looking for any port in a storm. What you have to show, clearly and without bombast, is how your qualifications and experience match the requirements of the job. You should not convey the impression that you can turn your hand to anything: this is a delusion of politicians, not practical businessmen.

Tailoring is the key. Proceed on the basis that the company knows what it needs and means what it says. For example, if the advertisement states a requirement for top level union negotiating experience, then you should be able to point to a good deal more than a few sporadic encounters with shopfloor representatives. Similarly, if the advertisement uses jargon which leaves you completely nonplussed, do not assume that it can be easily translated into more familiar terms (e.g. the applicant for a training job who thought that T-Groups were housewives' panels used in testing new products). But above all keep your letter brief. Many applicants appear to think that busy personnel people like nothing better than to curl up with a letter of Tolstoyan length as a welcome relief from their more mundane duties. Emphatically, this is not so. On the contrary, one of the most daunting chores for any personnel man is having to plough through the mass of turgid, ill-written, and frequently irrelevant applications which arrive after an advertisement in the national press. The few really thoughtful letters stand out like beacons.

Buckshot

It may well be that your arrival on the job market coincides with an economic recession or with a drop in demand for executives in your specialist field. Clearly, you cannot afford to wait for the right advertisements: you will either have to create some opportunities or be prepared to stagnate.

The art of writing unsolicited applications has many similarities with door-to-door salesmenship. You have no reason to believe that the 'prospect' actually needs what you are selling but you are going to try to interest him just the same. The key word, of course, is 'interest'. It is no use expecting him to be electrified by a ten-page CV which covers every aspect of your career in laborious detail: you need a rapier not a sledgehammer to penetrate his defences. This means that your letter must contain some unique point of interest for your reader which, hopefully, will make him feel that you might be worth a closer look. And this in turn means doing some research.

Fortunately, there is no lack of information about the problems and opportunities facing many UK companies, still less about their products and the markets in which they operate. As a regular discipline you should at least read the City pages of the quality dailies in addition to the Sunday business supplements and a good financial weekly. All of these sources, together with business directories such as *Kompass*, can provide you with many valuable 'leads' for your 'on spec' letter. For example, you may have read a news item about a company with ambitious plans for expanding into Europe: clearly it will be needing executives who can speak fluent French and German. If you happen to have such qualifications then obviously your letter is more likely to produce an interview than one which merely says, in effect, 'Please see me, I need a job'.

Nevertheless, even with the most careful research, you must be prepared for many disappointments: the mortality rate for this kind of letter is invariably high. But compared with the typical 'out of the blue' application at least you have a sporting chance. With the latter you need a miracle.

Mr Wonderful

Traditional British reserve, coupled with a certain distaste for self-advertising, has made many unemployed executives reluctant to publicize their availability by registering with the various executive employment agencies (including the much improved PER). Admittedly, it can be galling to have a lifetime of achievement reduced to one or two brief paragraphs but you cannot afford to ignore any possible pipeline to a new employer. Common sense dictates that the more lines you put out the more likely you are to catch a fish.

It is, of course, a very impersonal process and despite the trumpeting by some agencies about their 'thousands' of client firms you should not expect to be overwhelmed by a tidal wave of letters inviting you to interviews. Still, it will cost you nothing to register and if you have highly marketable skills it should not be too long before the trout begin to rise. However, if you are more entrepreneurially inclined, it could be worthwhile inserting an advertisement in the journal of your professional association or in the more widely read sections of the trade press for your industry.

The mistake which many executives make in such advertisements is to surround their qualifications with a veritable Berlin Wall of constraints

161

and prohibitions, particularly with regard to salary and status. To state 'salary required not less than £9000' or 'seeks board appointment with top hat pension' is not the most realistic way of attracting a potential employer. After all few men are indispensable in modern business and no one should know this better than an unemployed executive. All the more reason for him to convey attitudes of flexibility and open-mindedness than to appear isolated from the realities of his market situation.

A good personal advertisement must be *positive*. It should state what you *can* do, what your strengths are, and create the feeling that you enjoy a challenge. It should not be used as a vehicle for negotiating your terms of employment nor should it give the impression that you are unwilling to learn new tricks. Remember, you are in a *selling* situation: it is futile deliberately to 'play hard to get'.

Cosa nostra

Understandably, in these meritocratic times, the 'old boy net' is becoming less and less acceptable as a means of regaining one's place on the executive ladder. This means that you must approach your business contacts with subtlety and discretion. A blunt request for a job may only succeed in arousing your contact's sense of guilt and such a man is unlikely to exert himself in restoring your fortunes. It is better to adopt a more oblique approach, emphasizing that you are 'on the market' rather than unemployed. He can then feel that his efforts on your behalf are simply a praiseworthy attempt to prevent talent from being wasted.

Remember, too, that a network of contacts is not built up overnight. Even if you are currently prospering in your job it is worth while insuring yourself against possible future disaster. This means not only knowing the 'right people' but also knowing where they are to be found. For less than the annual cost of smoking 20 cigarettes a day you can become a member of a businessman's club or of a number of executive management institutions, all of which can provide you with valuable contacts. Many an unemployed executive has found a new niche over a pre-lunch gin and tonic at a management seminar or amid the chintzy surroundings of his institute's club. Like any other investment, such strategic socializing may take time to pay off but it is there when you need it—which may be sooner than you think.

Similarly, while you are still employed, think twice before you turn down invitations to speak at management conferences. By accepting, you will not only be proving your public spiritedness: you will also be gaining a valuable platform. It is not only obscure actors who can suddenly leap to fame through having been seen by the right producer. The same thing can happen to a managerial 'unknown' if he impresses a tycoon who may be in the audience. So be prepared occasionally to sing for your supper. It could lead to some useful entrées when you are down on your luck.

Safari

Doing the rounds of the headhunters and selection consultants is another worthwhile tactic, provided that you are reasonably selective in your choice of firms. For example, if you are a five thousand-a-year man, it is useless to contact the type of headhunter who is only interested in executives earning more than 10K. Nor should you pick a selection consultancy simply on the basis of its lively recruitment advertising: this may be more of a tribute to the imagination of the copywriter than an indicator of its efficiency in matching people with jobs. Once again, this is a legitimate opportunity for you to use your contacts, both to seek their advice regarding which firms to contact and to alert them to the fact that you are currently 'between jobs'.

When invited to interview, take care not to oversell yourself. If you are well known in your field, the consultant will almost certainly have a file on you; if not, then do not behave as though he has failed to do his homework. Bear in mind that the dividing line between brisk self-confidence and latent egomania can often appear extremely thin and that in this particular situation the consultant is buying, not selling. The impression which you must strive to give is of a man who is not only professionally competent but mature and flexible enough to appeal to a wide range of companies. You will certainly not achieve this if you appear to regard any suggestion of a job below board level as tantamount to a personal affront.

Most headhunters and selection consultants are compassionate men: indeed some of the best in the business have known the pangs of redundancy in their earlier careers. This will not prevent them from probing deeply into why it was *you*, rather than someone else, who was fired, retired early, or made redundant; and you had better have a credible explanation (on no account trot out that tired old cliché about 'policy differences'). It is best to 'come clean' rather than to become enmeshed in a web of half-truths. After all you are not being judged as a candidate for sainthood and it is absurd to pretend that you have never made a mistake.

Green pastures

Inside every organization man is an entrepreneur waiting to leap out,

163

or so it would appear judging by the numbers of unemployed executives who try to start their own businesses. Unfortunately, technical competence and enthusiasm, though important, are rarely enough to ensure survival. Not only do you need to find that elusive 'gap in the market': you also need a special brand of versatility and the kind of temperament which can tolerate uncertainty. You also need luck.

Make no mistake: the longer you have been employed (particularly in large organizations) the more difficulty you may have in adjusting to being a one-man band, responsible for your own production, marketing, accounting, and research. In fact, long before the axe falls, you should have laid contingency plans for just such a day by ferreting out as much information as possible about the business in which you are interested. Renting an office and calling yourself a consultant may be flattering to your ego but it will not keep you solvent. You need to talk to people who are knowledgeable about your intended field; to keep abreast of market trends; and, above all, to discuss those all-important financial questions with your bank manager or accountant.

Tired of the rat race, many former executives decide to embark upon a completely new career. Teaching 'management studies' is a particularly popular choice but once again such a move needs careful planning and a mature awareness of what will be involved. Not every executive has the mental resilience or indeed the communications skills to be a good teacher and the slower pace of academic life can sometimes be frustrating for a man who has been accustomed to a more strenuous environment. If you have never felt the urge to develop people or if you have not been used to having your ideas questioned, then you may find that lecturing is by no means a 'soft option'. Unhappily, those who can do frequently can't teach.

The same considerations apply to any other kind of radical departure from business life; for example, hospital administration or social work. The man who succeeds in adapting to a new career is often one with few illusions about his own temperament and personality.

Finding a new job is like fighting a battle: to succeed you need both a strategy and tactical skills. Of paramount importance is the need to cast your net wide and to be aggressive rather than passive in creating new opportunities. Above all, you must not become despondent because of disappointments and setbacks: these are bound to occur while you are testing the market. Essentially you need those same qualities of persistence and determination which, hopefully, you displayed when you were still employed. And you owe it to yourself not to give less than your best.

164

Further reading

Books will speak plain when counsellors blanch.

Francis Bacon, *Essay*

Battalia, William and John Tarrant, *The Corporate Eunuch*, Abelard-Schuman, 1974.

Cleverly, Graham, *Managers and Magic*, Longman, 1971.

Heller, Robert, *The Naked Manager*, Coronet, 1974.

Jay, Antony, *Management and Machiavelli*, Pelican, 1973.

Kelly, Al, *What to do and what not to do to make life easier for yourself at work*, McGraw-Hill, 1973.

Moreau, David, *Look Behind You!*, Associated Business Programmes, 1973.

Packard, Vance, *The Pyramid Climbers*, Pelican, 1965.

Parkinson, C. Northcote, *Parkinson's Law*, Murray, 1958.

Peter, Laurence and Raymond Hull, *The Peter Principle*, Pan, 1971.

Townsend, Robert, *Up the Organization*, Coronet, 1971.

Whyte, William H., *The Organization Man*, Penguin, 1960.

Printed in Great Britain at the Alden Press, Oxford